WORKING
IN
CANADA

WORKING

IN

CANADA

edited by Walter Johnson

BLACK ROSE BOOKS   Montréal

BLACK ROSE BOOKS No. E25

Hardcover — ISBN: 0-919618-64-2

Paperback — ISBN 0-919618-63-4

Canadian Cataloguing in Publication Data

Main entry under title:

Working in Canada

ISBN 0-919618-63-4 bd.
ISBN 0-919618-64-2 pa.

1. Industrial sociology. 2. Work.
1. Johnson, Walter, 1952-

HD8106.5.W67   301.5'5   C76-015023-0

Cover Design: Michael Carter
Cover Photograph: Olivia Rovinescu

Inside Photographs: Olivia Rovinesau and Clifton Ruggles

BLACK ROSE BOOKS LTD.
3934 rue St. Urbain
Montréal H2W 1V2, Québec

Printed and bound in Québec, Canada

305. 56 0971
W 926j
LW.201756

Contents

Preface

The publication of this book is, for me, the culmination of a process which began three years ago in an automobile factory north of Montreal. I had been working there for several years but with each passing year my sense of well-being was corroded by a work environment that degraded and made fools of everyone who was caught up in it. When I left school I tried the usual variety of jobs but eventually ended up in the car factory because it was close to home and the wages were the best around. Like most young people, I entered the workforce with energy and high aspirations. I could not possibly imagine then that within the next ten year period this energy would be dissipated and my adolescent aspirations would become a sour joke.

The factory system that I had entered seemed especially designed to take some of the best qualities and virtues of people (eagerness, the desire for personal efficacy, responsibility) and transform them into tools to be used for the repression, manipulation and domination of other workers. To learn anything important or "make something of oneself" one had to rise in the corporate hierarchy and to rise in the hierarchy meant committing a series of acts which demonstrated a feeling of contempt for fellow workmates and a cold-blooded talent for manipulation.

People who were incapable of performing these acts seldom advanced very far in the hierarchical corporate framework. This does not mean that there are not many fine people who work at all levels in the corporation but, under the existing circumstances, it is inevitable that the integrity of these people will be slowly chipped away by the behaviour modification which is necessary in order to survive in the corporate pecking order. It would be foolish, however, to get on a moral high horse and cast stones at people who are caught up in processes which, no matter how injurious to personal autonomy and self-esteem, are essential for their survival. Nevertheless, it is important, for those who can, to expose the absurdity and wrongheadedness of any situation so that changes might come about.

The way I chose to reveal and combat the stupidity that I witnessed daily in the automobile industry was through a personal resistance to arbitrary authority in the plant and by writing about my experiences to let the general public know what was going on.

Through my writing I became associated with a group of people in Montreal, the *Our Generation* and *Black Rose Books* editorial boards, who shared my dissatisfaction with industrial life as it is now constituted. My association with that group, and particularly two people in the group, Lucia Kowaluk and Dimitrios Roussopoulos, helped to strengthen my long-held belief that working in our society need not be a personality destroying and health debilitating experience. Through them I was introduced to many other people who also believe that a rational, productive and humanly satisfying work environment is not only possible but absolutely essential if our society is to progress and flourish. People like Harold Wilson and Gerry Hunnius who, rather than drop out of society in disillusionment, remain in the mainstream of life and attempt to provide some alternative to the outmoded and autocratic organisational techniques and activities of the large corporations. With this background and with the support of *Black Rose Books* I was encouraged to seek out and record the views of other workers who also felt that work in our society might be organized in a way which would develop peoples'full potential without continually rupturing that tenuous bond of social affection that is the hallmark of any truly civilized society. This book is the result of that search.

It should be understood that the contributors to this book are not professional writers so the quality and style of writing varies with each piece. Readers who are expecting a dazzling display of intellectual pyrotechnics should look elsewhere. All the contributors were encouraged from the very beginning to express themselves as they saw fit. A few preferred to be interviewed rather than to attempt to write lengthy pieces. Others chose to give a highly personalized account of their work and life experiences. I didn't discourage this because it makes for a good deal of diversity and individual analysis while also giving the reader some insight as to the character and personal background of the writer. I feel that this approach creates a more interesting book as well. There was, however, an effort to downplay the kind of radical chest thumping and verbal cholesterol that tend to weaken books of this nature. No conscious attempt was made to put forward a collective blueprint for a new society.

What does emerge from this book is a penetrating critique of modern industrial life from people who are directly involved in it. There is, of course, a good deal of griping about pet beefs and seemingly unimportant events but this is symptomatic of a larger problem which all the contributors identified and which is the central theme of this book: the belief that our society, meaning the business, bureaucratic and academic elites, has a vested interest in denying workers the kind of social approval which generates self-respect and enables people to demand a work environment where their sense of autonomy, dignity, and self-worth is recognized and valued. It is no accident that social approval is the one commodity denied to the working class. The ruling class knows that people who feel unworthy or inferior are more vulnerable to manipulation and easier to keep in place than people who have no doubts about their worth to society.

Social approval has not been extended to the working class because it is the most numerically significant force in society and therefore the biggest threat to the status quo should its energies be mobilized. It is easier to grant social esteem to an advertising executive than to a worker. The advertising executive represents no real threat to established order and, in fact, functions as one of the main props of a demoralized and disintegrating culture. Is it merely a coincidence that some of the most prestigious and highly paid jobs in our society are also the most transparently worthless? It is precisely because workers do the hard, shitty and necessary tasks in society that they cannot be given social approval. If workers were allowed to see their role as central to the functioning of society it would only be a matter of time before they would question the nature of the production process and the interests that it serves. This type of awareness is, and always has been, intolerable to the dominant elites and so they have, over a period of time, reified, through the educational process, the media, the church, and all hierarchical institutions promoting individual ascendancy, the notion that the working class, as a class, is inherently lacking in administrative ability, social skills, and a sense of responsibility, and is therefore unworthy of social esteem.

Unfortunately, much of the working class has, to an almost paralysing extent, accepted and internalized this image. We've been only too willing to delegate responsibility to the school board, the church, the union, the State, and the result has been a progressive diminution of self-esteem among the working class. Today there is some truth in the T.V. caricature of workers as television watchers, car buyers, beer drinkers and not much else. Every one of the contributors to this book stressed the importance of self-respect and self-assertiveness as pre-requisites for the revitalization of the working class.

As long as workers view themselves as second class citizens their influence and ability to change things in society will be minimal. Demands that workers should have more control over the work environment and decision-making process can only be achieved when workers believe such demands are legitimate. Most unions have discouraged demands of this kind by suggesting that workers are better served through the adversary system of labour-management relations. It is true that well organized unions can exert considerable leverage in economic matters but activities and authority on the shop floor remain the exclusive domain of management. Major contracts or collective agreements now drawn up seem specifically designed to define the rights and prerogatives of management (one militant in the automobile industry labelled the collective agreement as a Magna Carta for management). The wording of these contracts leaves no doubt as to who is boss and the so-called rights of workers seem more like the obligations of prisoners.

What is now being questioned by many workers, including the contributors to this book, is the legitimacy of managements' rights. At one time the function of management was to carry out the decisions that were made by the owners of the enterprise they worked for. With the evolution of capitalism and the development of large impersonal corporations the role of the owners (shareholders) became less important and more of the decision-making power was ceded to management. It was assumed that management had a pre-emptive right to make decisions by virtue of their close association with the owners and the expertise they accrued because of that association. This is now taken for granted even though a large proportion of the management of corporations is made up of people who have never met nor even come near the owners in their life. They are employees of the company who make decisions and create policies that affect other employees known as workers. Such power should not be concentrated in the hands of a few employees. Through the trade union process, and the structures that have been created, workers are increasingly capable of knowing as much as management does about the operations of an enterprise. It is therefore absurd that workers should be denied any longer the right to enter into the decision making process. The problem is that the very trade union structure that created the possibility of workers' control is now also the greatest obstacle to its fulfillment.

The established union hierarchy does not recognize control of the work environment or a role in the decision-making process as legitimate demands. Demands of this kind seem impractical to well ensconced labour bureaucrats who have made their reputations through the collective bargaining process. The fact is that a movement towards workers' control might threaten the existing union structure which is hierarchically oriented and resistant to change from below.

The resistance of unions to this evolutionary process is reminiscent of the quixotic battle which many old-fashioned capitalists and founding entrepreneurs engaged in to prevent their managers from assuming too much power in companies that had become too large for one-man control. The Ford Motor Company was almost ruined, in the thirties, by Henry Ford's unwillingness to share decision-making authority with his management team. The union movement might suffer the same fate if it continues to ignore the warning signals raised by radical rank and filers.

By substituting the word State for management all of the above arguments can also be applied to public service workers and the working poor. For this reason the book deals with the working class as it really exists, a mixed stew of industrial workers, public service workers, clerical workers and unorganized working poor. All have one thing in common: a desire for more control over their own lives. If it does nothing else this book should at least provide a glimpse into the lives of working people in Canada. It should help demolish the myth that workers in Canada are a contented, docile lot incapable of sustained thought or a radical critique.

On a larger scale this book is concerned not only with the work environment but the society we live in as well, the two being inextricably linked. Workers want to play an important role in society and to accomplish this they must create the appropriate organizations. There is, therefore, a political dimension to the book which I deal with in my concluding essay. Not all of the contributors would agree with my analysis of the evolution of the working class in Canada but they do respect my right as editor to draw such conclusions. It is now time to let the readers come to their own conclusions.

Walter Johnson

Working in the Post Office

by Peter Taylor

I really didn't like working at the post office. In fact, I hated it. After 9 months of working there, that is the only conclusion. Oh, the money was o.k., and I certainly liked some of the other workers, but when all is said and done, I hated work. And it wasn't simply the job itself, although sticking letters in pigeonholes isn't exactly the most fulfilling way to spend 8 hours a day. Much more than this, I hated work because of the kind of life it forced me to live 24 hours a day. Because, after a while, it became pretty clear that work affected just about everything I did away from work.

The shift I worked took my time from 9.45 p.m. to 6:15 a.m. So every night, some time before 9:45, along with about 400 other people, I would stop whatever I was doing and set out for work. Luckily, I lived close to work, so I could delay leaving until about 9:23. Some of my friends weren't so lucky — one even had to leave by 8 o'clock. But whatever time we left, they never started paying us until 9:45 or when we punched in — whichever was later.

Punching-in was probably the worst time of the day. Pushing down the card, waiting for the thud of the stamp to signal the beginning of another shift. It was just like entering a prison — at least that's how everybody looked. After seeing a friend drag herself up the stairs to our work area, I asked what was wrong. She simply said: "It's not 6:15 yet."

A couple of times, however, I managed to punch-in late — and get away with it! The best time I pulled this off was with another friend. We were both late, and while walking from the subway to the post office we agreed that a jammed subway door had caused our lateness. And figuring that a 15 minute breakdown sounded better than a 2 minute one, we took our time. In fact, we took our first "unofficial" break of the evening. After a cigarette and a good rap, we went upstairs to get the shift supervisor to sign our punch cards, went back downstairs to the card racks, went upstairs again to the work area

Peter Taylor is a former Post Office worker living and working in Toronto.

and then began to work. All in all we gained about 25 minutes at full pay.

Even when we punched-in on time we would always go to a break area — either a washroom or a smoking area. At 9:45 some people would leave for the work area — in order to find stools. Most of us stayed, however, until about 9:47, when a supervisor would come out to tell us for the first time that evening that "we were paid to work". After some verbal opposition, we'd wander out into the work area looking for stools.

And there were never enough to go around. It used to piss me off that although they could spend millions of dollars on the new postal machines, they wouldn't buy the extra couple of dozen stools we needed. So I always made sure there were never any unused stools anywhere on the floor. Criss-crossing the floor looking for a stool, I made good use of the time by talking to friends.

The work itself was totally mechanical. We'd sit, or stand, in front of a sorting case that contained about 80 pigeonholes. (Officially called "cases", we often referred to them as "cages".) It would take about 3 or 4 shifts to learn a case. After that, sorting required no thinking, just reflexes. I remember Johnny Bower, who used to be goal tender for the Toronto Maple Leafs, saying that after practice the stopping of a hockey puck became a reflex action, that the nerve impulse from his eye, without going to his brain, would cause his hand to move. Sorting mail was exactly the same: I'd scan the envelope for the street name, house number, and town, then move my hand to the appropriate pigeonhole.

This operation was repeated over and over: 25 times a minute, 1500 times an hour. Over and over, for 8 hours each night. When I applied for the job, they made me write both a memory test and an intelligence test. But in no way did the job require any skill, beyond a basic ability to read. The part-time sorters, who did the same job, weren't required to write either test and, in fact, some workers who had failed these tests were allowed to work while waiting to take them again. The whole exercise was a holdover from the time when sorting mail required a detailed knowledge of the postal system, and nobody seemed to believe in it any more. Another reason they bypassed this selection mechanism was that they had to — with turnover rates above 50%, they needed any workers they could get.

No thinking; just reflexes. It's often said that sorting mail is boring, but that bit of understatement just doesn't come at all close to describing the true situation. In the first place, I learned to forget what I was doing, as I was doing it. Given the speed we were supposed to work, I never really had time to read the address. Rather, I would run my eyes over the address looking for certain key words (like Toronto), certain key letters (the primary sort consisted in breaking down the mail alphabetically according to street name) and certain street numbers. After seeing these key sections of the address, I would deal the letter to the appropriate pigeonhole. By that time I would have forgotten the address. This "forgetting" was necessary because it took time for the next address and I found it easier if my mind was blank. And besides, who wants to remember 1500 anonymous addresses an hour? And so I learned to forget what I was reading. At the beginning I reacted to this by checking the case to see how I'd done — after a while I just didn't bother.

You could always daydream. In fact you find it necessary. Women, music, politics, time after work, all floated through my mind. Of course these images were totally unrelated to the actual work I was doing; I found myself working, and at the same time thinking, wishing, pretending I was somewhere else. Dope obviously helped. Like most large factories, lots of people were stoned or drunk much of the time. Hating work, wishing you were somewhere else, and yet finding yourself there each night....

Occasionally we would think about work. Or rather about how much better work could be. We all had our own ideas, and mine consisted of abolishing afternoon and night work (we can all afford to get our mail a day later); getting rid of all the bills (which nobody can afford anyway); and increasing our wages so we could afford to work a lot fewer hours. Besides, as a friend said: "With more time off, you'd spend more money."

When I was working at the "standard" rate of 25 letters a minute, my hand would always be moving. But if I got too absorbed in my daydreams, then my hand would stop. And as my hand stopped, my productivity would start to go down. For the supervisors, this was a real problem. Their job was to keep us working every minute, and as there was no official form of work measurement, they were reduced to watching our hands move. Any pause or hesitation, if spotted, usually invoked their second favourite saying: "Keep your hands moving."

There used to be a system of work measurement, but several years ago postal workers got together and had it abolished. Actually during the time I worked there they began a series of case checks which consisted of counting all the letters somebody had sorted in the preceding hour. But several grievances, some talking back, and widespread support for workers who had their cases counted, soon put an end to these checks.

Because they used our hand motion as a productivity counter, they kept a constant eye on all of us. In order to make this task easier, they had arranged the cases in long rows. Often they would simply stand at the end of the aisle — watching. And even when we couldn't see a supervisor, we could never tell when one of them would stick his head around the corner of the row. It was just like being kept under guard for 8 hours a day. And their system of "spy windows" only added to the prison-like atmosphere. Arranged so they covered the entire work area, these very narrow slits supposedly helped them stop some of us from supplementing our wages by sampling the cash, credit cards, dope, etc., that the mails carried. (In the new postal plants, they plan to use the "wonders of technology" by installing remote-controlled TV cameras.) The fascist-like atmosphere didn't go unnoticed — particularly the night the shift supervisor made the mistake of wearing a brown shirt.

The feeling of being spied on was particularly strong during the 6 month probationary period. First, the union, by officially refusing to stand by the probationary worker, eliminated the legal defence procedure. Secondly, because, when I started, I knew only one person casually, I knew I couldn't expect much support from a bunch of people I hardly knew and who hardly knew me. For both these reasons, the power of the supervisors loomed large and as a result I felt very vulnerable. And the 2 and 4 month efficiency (or progress) reports seemed to be used mainly as scare tactics. After a while, of course, as I got to know some of the other workers, I began to see how little real control the supervisors could actually exercise.

Nevertheless they did have some power. One thing they seemed to especially enjoy was splitting up friends. Because when people talked to each other they couldn't be forced to work as hard, they would constantly move us around. Obviously this made it more difficult to establish friendships, but this didn't seem to bother them — I think they would have been happier if we had all been robots. So they moved us around, here and there, as they pleased. Sometimes when they were directing us towards unused cases, they looked just like traffic cops, or parking lot attendants, or prison guards.

Our official breaks were also just as regimented. As in high school, they used bells to start and end these breaks. Unlike a high school, however, the bells weren't hooked up to a master clock, but were activated by a supervisor downstairs. The approach of break time caused a great deal of clock watching — all designed to prevent us from losing any break time. In fact, we would often stop working early and begin to make our way towards the cafeteria. This, of course, was discouraged by the supervisors, but they found it next to impossible to stop us from leaving our cases before the bell rang.

In part our leaving early was necessary because the 10 minute break hardly gave us enough time — considering the line-ups that formed in the cafeteria, which itself was located on another floor. Not that the food was good or anything. After eating their dinners for several months I found myself suddenly feeling very full just before lunch time. Overcooked vegetables, stale bread, dried out meat: after eating at the post office, McDonald's hamburgers actually began to look good!

Along with the poor food went the noise. Uncovered cement and brick walls don't absorb much sound, so we were treated to their echoes. I guess they figured covering the walls with a sound absorber would have been a poor way to spend money. They had painted the walls with large brightly coloured designs, presumably to "brighten" the place up, but it just made the walls look gaudy, which only added to the glare.

But in comparison to the tension, caused by the supervisors' constant surveillance, the cafeteria certainly came out ahead, the food and noise notwithstanding. At least during the breaks and over lunch I could relax a little, talk with my friends, play cards and maybe do a bit of reading. Some workers used the lunch break to leave the building. They'd go to the closest all-night restaurant. The food was better, and just the fact of leaving the building gave a sense of relief. But half an hour isn't very long — even if you stayed inside. Of course they didn't pay us for our lunch break. The fact that all of us were there only because of the work — and if we had a choice we would have been elsewhere — just didn't count for them. It was just the same as the time we spent travelling to and from work: for us it was a necessary part of the job; for them, because it was "after hours", it was considered "free time", and therefore unpaid.

The end of break times was announced by yet another ringing of the bells. Because we had to punch-in after lunch, we left the cafeteria on time, although even then some supervisors would loudly remind us it was time to leave — as if we needed reminding!

At the end of the break times, however, hardly anybody left on time. The bell would ring and we would just continue to sit there. The supervisors would begin yelling: "Let's go! Time's up!" But usually even this had only a limited effect. Considering what was waiting for us downstairs, it was a real effort for any of us to go back at all. And so the supervisors would walk over to the tables and begin to challenge us directly. More often than not, there would be some talking back, often in the form of belittling the supervisor personally. During the whole time I worked there, this scene was repeated every shift. Nobody ever had it together enough to refuse outright, but we all figured that if they wanted *us* to work, then *they* were going to have to work for it.

After break, while going back to work, our main concern was the length of time till the next break — and after the last break, there were only one and three-quarters hours till we finished. Actually we would only work for about an hour and 15 minutes, but we still had an hour and three-quarters until we could punch out.

During the winter months the night continued right past the time to punch-out. But when summer came, the sun rose shortly before the shift ended. I always looked forward to this event, hoping for one of those spectacular sunrises that often herald the coming day. The view itself wasn't that exciting — train yards, parking lots, expressways — but I always enjoyed seeing the light of day for the first time in 8 hours. But perhaps it was just because it announced the end of the shift.

Punching-out was the best time of the day. Impatiently, we would wait in line until 6:15. Then we would surge past the punch clock, half running down the stairs, getting our coats from the lockers, stepping outside: FREE. Another night done —another night gone. At 6:17 the morning rush hour hadn't started. So walking home along the almost deserted streets I relaxed for the first time since the shift had started. With the calm of the city providing a much needed relief from the tension of constant surveillance, from the pressure of forced work, I would try not to think about having to go back to work that evening.

But no matter how hard I tried, I could never really escape. Already the travelling time demanded by work took away some of my free time. Because I lived close to work, it only added about an hour to my work day; for other people, it added up to three hours a day. And if I was going to function even moderately well at work that night, I obviously had to get some sleep, eat some food, make sure I had some clean clothes, etc. Not that I would have stopped sleeping and eating if I had stopped working, but in that case I would do these things to renew my energy for my own activities instead of for work. Work also determined *when* I could eat and sleep — one of the greatest benefits of quitting was regaining the possibility of sleeping at night. So laundry, food, sleep, shopping, errands, all conspired to take away most of my free time. Even before I reached home, my day, which on leaving work had stretched so invitingly before me, began to disappear behind the time taken by those chores required just to keep me going.

As a result, my time became very precious. Already a clock-watcher at work, now, in a vain attempt to preserve my free time, I began to clock-watch at home. At work, where the clocks told me how long until I could leave, they never seemed to move fast enough; at home, where they ticked away the time until I re-entered the factory, they moved at a speed which more than made up for their lethargy at work. To gain more free time I cut down on my sleep. I slept only 5 or 6 hours a day, but it really didn't make that much difference. There was never enough time. And even when I had gained some free time, my head, knowing that in a few short hours I had to go back, was never free. Long before I was ready, it would be time to go back to work.

20

And work didn't just steal my time. It also sabotaged my friend-ships. If friendships are to grow and develop, they require time — and work certainly left very little of that. Second, because most of my friends (and most people in general) worked days and I worked nights, I found myself "out of step". My friends, after working during the day, would spend the time after dinner relaxing; I would spend the same time trying to "psych" myself up for work. In the morning, when I had finished work, they would either be sleeping, or rushing off to work. Sleeping when most people were up and about; working when most people were sleeping; losing any semblance of "night life": work pressed my life into a topsy-turvy world.

My relationships with women also suffered. First of all, work prohibited me from making love at night. Before I started working at the post office, that had seemed perfectly normal. Now, under the "rules of work", it was forbidden. And if I took time off to satisfy my needs, then they would impose penalties in the form of suspensions and ultimately firing. Even being able to relax with women was, for most nights, completely out of the question — even though half my shift was made up of women. With all the pressure of management's "spy-system", everybody was on edge. So it was difficult to feel at ease and, as a result, it was hard to get to know each other. This obviously affected my relationships with men as well, but somehow it seemed to interfere more with my relationships with women.

The "guys downstairs" in the Traffic department were forced to spend most of their evenings and nights without even seeing a woman. This certainly made it more difficult for them to feel at ease with women after work. Towards my girlfriend I became much more demanding. Feeling the pressure and tension of work, I put pressure on her. Not only did my sexual needs come first, but it was my problems and my feelings which received the most attention. For her, I gave less support. My friends have said that work affected them in much the same way. Considering how segregated most workplaces are, it's not surprising that relationships between men and women are so messed up.

Evenings were the worst time, because then work imposed *its* timetable most ruthlessly. Along with a number of friends, I used to go to a pub about once a week. We'd go about 9 and stay till closing. In fact it became a bit of a social institution. But work put an end to all that. And so, as they would wander off to the pub, I'd go off to punch-in. Over a period of time, unable to keep contact, I found myself getting more and more isolated.

Work undermined my friendships in yet another way. An integral part of most relationships is having common experiences, doing things together. But most of my friends didn't work at the post office. That's the way things are organized in this society. When you apply for a job, you do it alone, as an individual, not with a group of your friends.

21

Work probably took more time than anything else, and it certainly was my most depressing activity. But because my friends didn't share my work experience, the amount of support I could get from them was obviously reduced. On the other side of the coin, dominated by work, taken up by events there, I was less able to provide support for them.

Shortly after I started working at the post office, a friend there told a supervisor to "Fuck off!" Needless to say, this was quite an event. Even after he quit, we would refer to him as "the guy who told Harvey (the supervisor) to fuck off." And knowing Harvey, we all thought it was really right-on — the only problem being that he got disciplined. (I think he put his disciplinary letter up in his bathroom.) But for my friends outside work, caught up by the pressure of their own work, this incident just didn't mean that much.

Over a period of time, the lack of time, the opposite schedules, and the different experiences, all combined to force us apart. I found my circle of friends reduced. Whereas I had been regularly spending time with about a dozen people, work cut this number down to 2 or 3. My work-friends had the same experience. For all of them, work meant spending less time with their friends.

Even when I slept, work would pursue me. After working about 2 months, I had my first dream about the post office. I was sitting in front of a case trying to sort the mail. But every time I moved my hand towards the right pigeonhole, the letter would just drift away. So I'd try again — and get the same result. Over and over I tried, never managing to put a letter in the case but at the same time, for some reason, I couldn't stop either. Finally I woke up. Everybody at work, at least everybody I talked to, had also dreamed about the post office. The dreams were all different, but two themes seemed to run through them all. First, we couldn't sort properly, and second, we had to keep trying. Although we always called them "dreams", they were really nightmares, but I guess it was just too heavy to admit that work gave us nightmares.

I remember talking with a number of workfriends about work and the effect it was having on us. We all agreed it was making us irritable, was cutting us off from our friends, was dulling both our senses and our minds, and was attacking our self-confidence. (After all, being forced to do something you hate and you *know* is a waste of time doesn't exactly improve your belief in your ability to handle the situation). But all these problems seemed to us to be simply the result of the way this society has organized our whole life around work. Both on and off the job, we are subject to a system of rules and regulations which seem designed to distort our lives — at least that is the major effect it has on us. In fact, all the institutions of this society — schools, family, government training programs, and so on — seem designed to make us ready, able and willing *workers*.

On the job itself, the supervisors weren't the major problem — or rather, they were the problem only to the extent that they insisted on enforcing the rules. Like most places, there were "good" and "bad" supervisors, and the difference between them was exactly how much they pushed us, how much they believed in this system of work. Management always claimed that this was the most efficient way to organize work, but we all knew it wasn't very efficient for *us*.

Of course we only worked for the money, but with inflation and everything, the next pay-day seemed to come around just in time. To get ahead, to save up any money was next to impossible. So most of us were forced to work — we had no choice. With taxes, rents, food prices, etc., eating up our hard-earned money, we were inevitably forced back to work. And we all agreed that we couldn't possibly buy enough to come close to making up for the life work forced us to live. In fact, no matter how much they paid us, we didn't think it could ever really be enough. After all, money doesn't buy back lost time. Writing about a hundred years ago in London, Karl Marx said that in capitalist society workers exchanged their creative power, their ability to live, for the money necessary just to survive, just to get them back to work. I think he hit the nail right on the head.

None of us, if we could do anything about it, planned to spend the rest of our lives at the post office. During the time I was there, several people retired. After spending 15, 20, 30 years of their lives working nights, they were finally leaving. We always stopped work and had a small ceremony. They'd get a small present from management and maybe a bit of money — and a lot of thanks. It just wasn't worth it. It wasn't, as they say, the way I was going to spend my life.

So I quit. And I wasn't alone; people were leaving all the time. When I started, the turnover rate was about 50% a year, that is, half the people who had started in the last year had quit. By the time I left, the pace had picked up considerably. People who had worked there for several years were saying that more people were leaving than ever before. One supervisor even said that the turnover rate had reached 80%!

For management, the high turnover was a real problem. (It seems that almost everything we enjoyed doing, they considered to be a problem.) They didn't like our leaving for two reasons. First, it meant they couldn't be very selective and had to hire just about anybody who came along. Second, because we were leaving anyway, the threat of firing lost a lot of its force. For both reasons they found it difficult to make us work hard. And we certainly weren't into helping them!

For if I quit work because I refused to live the kind of life it forced on me, then I also refused, as best I could, to live that life even while I was working. Every night I worked was a night lost forever. If they were to try to take my life away from me, then they weren't going to get away with it without a fight that would cost them as much as possible.

Because they were fooling around with *my life,* I felt more strongly about this than practically anything else. All the more so because if they had been willing to spend a bit more money, then it would have been quite different. (For example, we worked nights because: a) big business and government saved money by having next day delivery; b) the government saved money by having two shifts use the same equipment and facilities. In comparison to what working nights does to your life, the extra money involved in: a) getting the mail out a day later; and b) buying an extra several hundred cases and more space, would have been more than well spent. Interestingly enough, when the new postal plants are opened up, they plan to *increase* the number of people working afternoons and nights.)

We all seemed to think the same way. Certainly we all spent a great deal of time getting back as much as we could. Oh, there was the occasional person who was into working — like the unskilled guy who was about 40 and had 9 kids — but they were just overwhelmingly outnumbered by the rest of us. The only time I ever heard the word "liberated" was in this connection. One guy, who had really been into working when he started three years ago, had over that time come to the conclusion that working hard just wouldn't get him anywhere. And so he decided to just relax, take as much time as he could, and enjoy it. In comparison to how he felt before, he said that now he felt "liberated". Obviously he wasn't really liberated as long as he was forced to work at all, but when I left, he was planning to do something about that. In this whole process, he was strongly supported by his workfriends. In fact, our struggles against work were one of the few things about work which gained our enthusiasm. And this feeling was tempered only by our concern not to overstep the limits of our power.

Most relationships at work were based simply on the fact we all worked at the same place. As you got to know people better, you found that you had other things in common, but for a long time work was the major reference point. This was especially true at the post office because, with the high turnover rates, people were leaving all the time. In most ways, however, working didn't provide a very good basis for relationships. First, because we exercised so little control while working, very little of us "came through". After all, robots don't have much of a personality. Second, people are more attractive, more interesting when they're doing something they enjoy — and none of us enjoyed working.

In contrast, our struggles against work provided a much better basis for relationships. First, because they were enjoyable — certainly enthusiasm. Second, because we had to do it ourselves — no "representative" (for example, the union) could do it for us — through them we could exercise some control over ourselves. Third, because all of us were engaged to some extent, there was a real feeling of being together against management. Caught as we were in a system where our needs came out last every time, our struggle against work was the one way we could "be ourselves", could act on our needs, could affirm our presence and importance. Thus taking a night off, taking "unofficial" breaks, talking back, refusing orders, etc. all generated enthusiasm, pleasure and support. Hating work, and feeling the need to fight back, I found this support expressed in both actions and words, to be the best thing in the whole post office.

And it certainly wasn't just limited to the men. Because women made up about half my shift, it was clear that if they weren't in favour of something, then it just didn't happen. But they were certainly into the struggle against work. After being without a woman supervisor for several months, management found it necessary to appoint one. After all, the male supervisors couldn't cover the women's washrooms very well!

I think it was the equal participation by women in the struggle against work which accounted for the degree of equality in relationships between men and women on my shift. Of course in many ways the men did have more power, but compared to other places I've worked, the women put up with a lot fewer hassles. In fact comments about a woman's body usually envoked a very cold, "Fuck off, buddy". There were a number of reasons for the power of the women: they received equal pay; they did (and didn't do) the same work; they made up half the shift. And then there's the existence of the women's movement. But after all these, still the most basic reason for the degree of equality between men and women was our equal participation in the struggle against work.

One of the more effective ways we fought against their system of work was by taking a night off when we wanted to. Even now I can vividly remember the pleasure, the sense of relief, that followed my calling in sick. With that phone call I would have gained a free evening. We used this time to do different things. Sometimes it would be a rock concert or a movie, other times it would be just to be with friends or to sleep. But all these activities had one thing in common: we felt they were more important than working.

On returning to work after being absent, we had to get our punch-cards from the office. During the summer, because so many of us decided to enjoy the evenings outside, there would be a line-up outside the office just before 9:45. Coming to work it was nice to see that other people were taking time off too. According to the contract, we would

25

get paid for 15 sick days a year (8 with a doctor's note; 7 without one). And so we were a very sickly lot. Practically every night one or another of my work-friends would be absent. My guess is that absenteeism ran somewhere around 10% a night, although on one Friday night about two-thirds of my shift just didn't bother to show up.

Another way we could take time off and get paid for it was called "court leave". This meant that we would get paid if: a) we were on jury duty; or b) if we produced proof that we had been in court with the purpose of testifying. Since we didn't actually have to testify, it was possible to go to court with a friend and then get the court clerk to state that you had been an "uncalled witness". As one person said: "It's a choice between 3 or 4 hours in court and 8½ hours at work."

In another department, the people went about taking time off with pay in a more organized way. Thirty minutes before the end of their shift, about half the people would just leave! Of course they couldn't just stride out the front door, but they had discovered many "escape" routes which led from the work areas to the outside. As one of them said: "We're only paid to be here for 8 hours, so there is no way I'm going to stay a minute longer." Many workers took turns staying back to punch the cards of the ones who left early. In the same department, people also made a practice of getting sick just past the 6½ hour mark of their shift. The contract says we would get paid for the full 8 hours if we punched out sick after 6½ hours — without losing any of the 15 days paid sick time. So regularly these workers got their travelling time paid for — and then some. On my shift, this tactic wasn't as interesting., because not much is happening at 4:15 a.m.

The list of ways to take time off and still get paid for it is endless. Just one more example: by taking time off during the week and then working a day's overtime, you could get paid for 44 hours while actually working 40 hours! In this case, you get paid more for working the same hours, but since we wanted to work as little as possible and get paid as much as possible, it works out to be better for us.

Most of the time, however, the struggle against work was actually conducted right on the shop floor. Long before I started working at the post office, workers had set up a system of "unofficial" breaks. Not recognized in the contract, their establishment and maintenance depended entirely on the relative power of the workers and the supervisors. During the time I worked there, there was an uneasy balance of about 10 minutes an hour in force. Often of course we would take longer, but 10 minutes usually didn't provoke any hassles from the supervisors.

Originally these breaks had been taken in the washrooms, but since this is a difficult place to police, management had set up a special smoking room. And we often used to take our breaks in the stairwells. Any place, in fact, where we could get away from the watchful eyes of the supervisors was used as a break area.

We often used to take breaks together, using the time to talk with our friends. The supervisors didn't like the idea of us taking breaks together. They lectured us several times, saying it looked bad if a lot of cases were vacant at the same time; we thought they were upset because it was harder for them to hassle somebody if they were in a group. They used to time us as well. On leaving the work area we would often notice a supervisor glancing down at his watch. And if you were particularly tardy, or if he didn't like you for some reason or other, he would come around afterwards just to hassle you.

They also used to raid the washrooms and smoking areas all the time. These raids would provide the occasion for often heated exchanges. Most of us claimed we had just arrived, while they would insist that we had taken enough time. One guy was particularly good at needling the supervisors. As a supervisor came over to tell us to go back, he would say in a loud voice: "Oh look, our waiter's coming! I'd like a steak, medium rare, of course..." Sometimes the supervisors would turn red and just walk away! Usually, however, they would try to ignore these comments and tell us to GET OUT.

Sitting outside the washroom provided an excellent view. First the supervisor would disappear into the washroom only to reappear a few minutes later, tight-lipped and wearing a scowl. After a suitable interval, he would be followed by up to 20 people who would be laughing and joking with one another. Then in another minute or so, more people in one's and two's would begin to drift back into the washroom. In some ways it was just like a battle for control of the washroom.

One time, because a supervisor had really hassled a worker, we decided to have a shit-in. Although it was poorly organized, about 35 of us ended up just standing around waiting for the stalls to open up. The supervisors came, and after some talking back and forth some people went back. The rest of us just stayed there until we had finished our business.

Even when we were sorting, we would often refuse to go along with their plan. Talking and stopping work as much as we could was only one way. Another was missorting. Usually this was not done deliberately — it was just a lot easier than being careful. But sometimes — especially during the slowdown which was organized to defend a shop steward who had been fired — missorting was quite deliberate. And apparently workers in other post offices were into the same thing. I remember getting a series of letters destined for France that had been mailed in Boston! Dutifully I sorted them on — after adding "via Toronto" to the address.

For some workers, including some who took an active part, the amount of "dogging it" was a cause of concern. While often enjoying their unofficial breaks, they would decry the lack of enthusiasm displayed towards work and warn that "if people didn't start working harder, then the whole system was in trouble." While this is true, I think their warnings were more rooted in their fear of provoking a crack down by the supervisors. Certainly through their actions, since they stopped work about as much as the rest of us, they demonstrated little concern for the "system".

Every night *all* of us used most of these tactics. So much so, that as well as looking like a prison, the post office also resembled a battlefield. Each night was filled with incidents, actions, and reactions, all designed to gain an advantage. For us, the aim was more money for less work; the supervisors and management obviously had the opposite goal. And over the years we've had some success.

Speaking to the Vancouver Board of Trade in April 1972, the Postmaster General said:

> "It is surprising to note that since our employees have been provided with better working conditions and higher salaries, since 1965 to be exact, the productivity index at the Post Office has fallen by 12.5%... To compensate for this drop in productivity, we had to hire more people; this represents an additional expenditure of nearly $17 million. Obviously, this state of affairs cannot continue. It would be totally illogical to think that the Post Office will continue to absorb the cost of this loss of productivity, inflating its deficit by taking on employees who, under normal circumstances, would not be needed."

In short, the post office is faced with workers who are working less and getting paid more. Significantly, the introduction of the new postal system is designed to "correct" this situation by making postal workers work harder and by reducing their wage levels. But it seems to me that the workers will be able to deal with this, just as they have pretty successfully dealt with all of management's ploys over the past few years.

But regardless of such far-reaching implications, for the most part our struggles were buried inside the post office, far from the public eye. To be sure, postal workers are not generally considered to be the hardest-working of workers, but with most of the mail moving reasonably quickly, little thought is given to the situation of the people who move the mail. All this changes when postal workers stop work altogether in a strike.

During the 9 months I worked there we had 2 strikes. Both times front page articles recorded the strike events. Editorials, noting the personal and particularly the financial inconvenience, made ringing statements about "essential services" and threats of "anarchy". And the TV news dutifully showed shots of piled mail bags and picket lines. In many ways though, these strikes were only a continuation of the daily struggle against work. Certainly the constant tension between needing the money and hating the work was still present, and played a major role in determining how we viewed strikes.

First, being on strike was like having a holiday. We could sleep at night, see our friends, and since we were all doing it together we didn't really have to worry about being disciplined. On returning to work after the 2 week strike in April, the question on everyone's lips was, "How was your holiday?" And even after we'd been back only a couple of hours, we were talking about the need for another "holiday" — soon.

On the other hand, being on strike meant losing money. None of us was happy about this, and with few exceptions, any desire to have the job reflected our need for money, not an interest in working. As one guy put it: "I don't care if this fucking place burns down; but I just started and I need the money to pay the rent." Both times I went on strike it was illegal, but this had little effect; after all, we'd broken the law before. No, the major consideration was whether we could pull it off, whether we could afford it.

In other ways, of course, being on strike was different. First, it was an escalation of our daily struggle because we were all acting together. On the shop floor, *all* of us took nights off, took breaks, etc., but we did it more as individuals, rather than in unison. In part this was because we were less visible and therefore less vulnerable when we didn't co-ordinate our actions too much; in part because each of us preferred to take different nights off, take breaks at different times, etc. Obviously these struggles had some effect, but during a strike, because we acted together, our effect was much greater. About 48% of all the mail in Canada passes through the main Toronto post office, so even a short work stoppage puts enormous pressure on management. My shift was solid during both strikes, and in part this accounts for the lack of disciplinary action taken against us.

Second, being on strike was different, because of the involvement of the union. On the shop floor, our struggles were conducted almost totally outside the union. Of course we would file grievances, but usually they were designed more to hassle management than actually to make any gains. For that, we relied on ourselves and each other.

During a strike, however, the presence of the union made itself felt. In part this was useful because, if the union officials supported a strike, then we were in a much stronger position. But the union's prominence during strikes was also a drawback in that they would try to run the show. In this respect they were sort of like supervisors who were always telling us what we could and couldn't do. The union officials preferred it when we just followed their orders, but since there was never any strike pay, their orders usually left us cold. Besides, the union's orders never amounted to much — the union officials by their actions made it all the more likely that we would simply take a "holiday" during a strike.

When a strike was over, the situation would quickly return to normal: the newspaper headlines would change to other topics, the union would retreat into its offices and meetings, and on the shop floor the struggle against work would resume. Even on the first night back, fresh from the time off, we would be taking breaks, talking back — just like before. If anything, the time off just made it that much harder to fit back in. And so day in and day out, right up until I quit, this struggle continued.

On my last night, after coming in late, I spent the time walking around saying goodbye to my friends, and just looking at the place where I'd spent so much time in the last 9 months. Even on the last night, I was hassled by the supervisor: "I know it's your last night, but you're being paid to work." Saying goodbye to my friends was the hardest part of leaving. Over the time I worked there I had gotten to know some people pretty well — we'd been through a lot and had fought back together on numerous occasions. And now, if my leaving was at all like that of others, I probably wouldn't see most of them again. Still the need to quit the post office was stronger. Walking down the ramp to the door for the last time, I could hardly believe the sense of relief I felt.

But at best, it's only a temporary reprieve. My next job will probably put me back in much the same kind of situation. And as long as even one of my friends is working at the post office, I'm still affected by it. A few weeks ago I went out drinking with a friend from the post office — he took the night off! Most of our discussion centred around work — or rather, around recent incidents in the struggle against work. And as we talked, it became very clear that neither of us would really be satisfied unti we "never had to go back again — ever".

P.S.

This article concentrated on the situation of young, single workers. As such, it described in detail the ways they fight against work. For example, the writer's decision to end his "tour of duty" after 9 months has been done by so many other people that management is faced with a permanent shortage of workers. This, in turn, has enabled people who stay on the job to resist management's attempts to get them to work harder — they can't just go around firing people, because somebody has to be left to keep at least *some* of the mail moving, however, slowly!

But if the young, single worker can resist in certain ways, it is clear that almost everybody at the post office also struggles against work — struggles for more money for less work. (Supervisors excepted, of course.) Workers on days, for example, are "masters at dogging it". Using their experience and their willingness to stick together in working less, they have managed to cut their work load by more than half over the years.

Taken together, the permanent slowdown by day workers and the upfront refusal to work by workers on afternoons and nights have given management quite a headache. And when you think that the struggle against work is going on in every post office in the country, it's no wonder Postmaster-General Mackasey is "concerned". The strength of all postal workers in the last few years — working less and getting more money — has forced the government to spend millions of dollars to introduce the new machines. As Mackasey told the Toronto Star : "We have to automate. We have to be able to handle increasing volumes of mail efficiently... It is imperative the post office function."

For them, "efficiently" means to decrease wages by de-classifying most jobs and cutting back on the number of workers hired. It also means to get more work out of the people who stay or will be hired at the new plants — for example, by trying to make people work at the speed of the machines, like the coding machines, which have automatic timers. *In other words, they plan to use the new postal system to get more for less money.*

Struggling against work is something postal workers have in common with each other. And it is also something they have in common with the rest of the working class. In practically every factory, office, school and home, people are working less and trying to get more money. Over the last few years, the big question in the business papers of North America and Europe is how to keep wage gains down, how to get workers to work harder, how to increase profits. In some ways, this is what they hope to accomplish through the ridiculously high rate of inflation. And workers are also increasing their struggle for more money for less work. In Canada, people have been stopping work to demand more money at a record rate. With inflation going even higher, it's likely things will heat up even more.

Working in an Auto Plant

interview with Claude Petelle

Johnson:
What are you doing at the plant right now?

Petelle:
I'm working on the assembly line now, sub-assembly on the door line putting wires in the doors before they reach the main line.

Johnson:
Are you still involved with the union?

Petelle:
Well, I'm still a good member but I'm no longer on the executive. I don't have any official titles whatsoever and I don't want any. It's a trap.

Johnson:
How long has it been since you've been on the executive?

Petelle:
It's been three years now. Since 1972, if I remember correctly.

Johnson:
And you haven't been a committeeman since then either. What happened?

Petelle:
I just didn't run for re-election, that's all. In my opinion, being an expert, and that's how people regarded me, is a handicap for the workers because I always had to go to the rank and file workers on the shop floor and tell them that they didn't have any problems. And I became tired of being the guy who has to tell the workers that they don't have any problems, because I know otherwise. It's absurd to tell people that they don't have problems simply because none of their problems are covered in the union contract or master agreement. I was caught in a position where, after six years, I had a certain amount of experience,

---

Claude Petelle works on the sub-assembly line at the General Motors plant in Ste. Therese, Québec. He was on the union executive there for six years.

through reading the agreement and applying its principles, and I couldn't do it any more, because I felt that the book, the agreement that is, was crippling the rank and file workers rather than helping them, even though it was workers who signed the goddamn agreement.

Johnson:
You felt that the contract, the master agreement, was really an agreement which favoured or benefited management rather than rank and file workers.

Petelle:
There's no doubt about it. Any agreement signed between management and workers in any goddamn country that I know of is a form of slavery as far as I'm concerned.

Johnson:
Why?

Petelle:
If a company is in business to make money it will try to attach the workers to a set of rules which will ensure that the flow of profits is as uninterrupted as possible. What the company does is to make certain concessions to the workers in matters concerning wages and fringe benefits but the work environment itself is disregarded by the union in favour of the company, so the company pretends that it is forced into accepting the financial demands of the union. And the worker is placed in the position of accepting higher wages as the only legitimate demand. The basic problems of the work environment are ignored.

Johnson:
But don't you think that some of the clauses in the contract protect workers under certain circumstances? For example, if a worker tells his foreman off, or if he yells at his foreman, or even if he slugs his foreman in the face?

Petelle:
No protection at all.

Johnson:
What about the arbitration process?

Petelle:
As far as I'm concerned the arbitration process is one of the most unjust procedures that workers must suffer through. In most cases the worker is condemned before he's judged! During the arbitration process the worker is forced to exist without his regular means of support. He's not allowed to work and often has to wait as long as two years before

a judgement is handed down. The company has got nothing to lose as they just throw the guy out and they wait for a judge to decide. And about ninety percent of the time, the judge is a guy who went to school with the bosses, comes from the same social stratum, goes to the same golf courses, drinks in the same nightclubs and sleeps with the same whores. He doesn't know what it means to be a worker.

Johnson:
Can you remember the percentage of cases that went to arbitration and were settled in management's favour? Can you recall that?

Petelle:
Over eighty percent.

Johnson:
That much?

Petelle:
Oh yeah. The majority of cases that I recall favoured the company. It couldn't be otherwise. If the worker is relying on arbitration to solve his problems he's out of touch with reality. And frankly, the company hopes that the worker believes in the arbitration process. It takes the heat off them.

Johnson:
Well surely, the workers are represented by the union executive when the contract is being drawn up? Why can't we have an agreement that's more favourable to rank and file workers in the plant. What are the obstacles?

Petelle:
It's like anything else in our society. The worker is delegating his power to a small minority of people, the union executive, who don't understand what the real problems are. I know what you're going to say, that most of the union reps or union business agents are from the working class. And it's true. But they tend to forget very goddamn fast about the problems of the rank and file because they're working in air conditioned offices, they're driving big cars, they have expense accounts. They're like bosses, and this is the main reason why the system operates against the real interests of the working class. The union reps are elevated to a position above ordinary workers. So how can they be for the workers if they're not with the workers. They're not experiencing the day to day problems of the workers. Our society is constructed like a triangle. At the top of the triangle, a small minority of people make the decisions for the great unwashed at the bottom of the triangle.

Johnson:

When a worker is elevated into a position of authority over his fellow workers he very soon assumes the attitudes of the bosses. He becomes a person who supposedly represents workers but, in reality, dominates them much the same as management does.

Petelle:

Definitely, there's no doubt about it. And you can go to Russia and it's the same thing. For a long time many people thought it was the perfect society but it's just as evident there that "the masses" take no part in the decision-making process. And it was supposed to be the perfect structure for a society. Well, I don't believe it. Neither the so-called capitalist societies, nor the so-called communist societies consult with ordinary working people. And in both societies the workers have just not set up the right kind of pattern to protect themselves.

Johnson:

What is the stumbling block that prevents the development of a working class consciousness?

Petelle:

It's very simple. Look, I was raised in the Montréal area and most of our fathers were trying to send us to school to have a better education so we wouldn't become "goddamn" workers. So if workers themselves feel that their kids should never be workers, how could a kid, when he grows up, believe that being a worker is worthwhile? It's an inferiority complex that is carried through the working class. The values of our society are screwed up badly. The people who are producing, who are doing the real work in our society, are the lowest paid in the scale of wages, they're the lowest in prestige. But remember that, in our society, money is also prestige. Money can buy you a degree of prestige, but the people who work the most in real terms, are the lowest paid. So how can you have a just society when the people who are *watching* the workers doing their jobs are also the highest paid and have the most prestige! It's absurd. It's nonsense.

Johnson:

We've been conditioned, by our upbringing and education, to believe that manual workers are not worth as much as some guy who's pushing paper or some guy who is supposedly superior simply because he has a clean job and a little bit of authority.

Petelle:

I know what you're saying and what I'm saying, in essence, is that if you don't respect yourself, you can't really expect to be respected by others.

Johnson:
Do you think that this lack of self-respect makes it easier for workers to be manipulated? Because a worker is trying to achieve a kind of respect in the eyes of someone he looks to as his superior, he tends to ingratiate himself to that person to gain some respect and is thus more susceptible to manipulation.

Petelle:
That's true, and not only to be manipulated but also to be a stool pigeon or any of the things people were not born to be. This goddamn society has all the answers when it comes to controlling people. The people are being controlled as much as they allow themselves to be controlled. This is it Christ, there are no machine guns at people's backs. People are being controlled by institutions like the family and also by the creation of false wants and needs. A person could end up with three T.V.'s, three cars and even three houses. Workers become part of the rat race. At least the old-fashioned slaves were bound by iron chains and when they broke their chains, they were free, but workers, the slaves of today, have chains made of gold and they don't want to break their chains. On the contrary, we want to keep our chains because we can't envision any alternatives to this rat race for commodities.

Johnson:
We're captives of our own upbringing and mentality.

Petelle:
Exactly. Captives because of the way we were raised and educated. The powerful in this society are not stupid. When we were in school we were not taught anything about unions, about governments, about what we had to face as workers. We were taught how to count, we learned how to add and subtract and these skills are primarily used to screw people. You don't need mathematics to tell a guy that you have three children, you just name them for Christ's sake. We're living in a society which values the wrong things. We don't give a damn whether we're polluting the air or the water. If it's a company, it's O.K.

Johnson:
If you're in a position of power you can get away with as much anti-social behaviour as you want, but if you're a worker and you indulge in anti-social behaviour the full weight of the law comes down on you. A worker, as an individual, is more easily condemned by the society and by the judges. This is proved every day in the courts when the judges take a worker and make an example of him while an executive or a powerful corporation can get away with real anti-social behaviour. Things haven't changed that much from the days of Jean Valjean in *Les Misérables*.

Petelle:
But remember that the judges are the same people as the arbitrators.
They went to the same schools, they go to the same golf courses and
they sleep with the same whores. This goddamn class is protecting
itself and we, as workers, can't blame them because we, as a class,
should be doing the same thing for ourselves. But we're not. We're
standing around looking at our navel or we're stabbing each other in
the back. The system is creating French-English battles, Protestant-
Catholic battles, black and white battles and while we are arguing on
sentimental or emotional issues, we're letting a powerful minority get
away with what they want.

Johnson:
And always, with these highly charged racial, ethnic or sectarian
conflicts, it's one element of the working class pitted against another
element of the working class. The people who are fighting are English
and French speaking working class people who take this emotional
issue and deal with it at the work place, where both groups are oppressed. But because it's been cranked up by the media, you have this
conflict developing. They're the people who work together and have to
deal with each other on a personal level. They're the ones who have
the arguments. It's not a French-Canadian working class person and a
guy from Upper Westmount that ever argue or discuss these things.

Petelle:
Yes, that's quite true but, on the other hand, it's evident that in Québec
the ruling power is in the hands of a minority that's English speaking.
They are the governing power because they have the economic power
and they don't want to lose it. And they'll do whatever is necessary
to keep that power. But it's true that the battle is fought between
workers of different languages because emotional or sentimental issues
affect people the most. Hitler knew that fact and used it to his advantage. And you can see this in capitalist society as well because
the working class must remain divided. As Che Guevara once said,
"Create a hundred Vietnams", but Che Guevara hadn't discovered
anything original when he said that. The capitalist system was doing
that a long time before Che Guevara said that and they keep doing it
all the time.

Johnson:
Claude, you've said before that you considered the union part of the
problem. You were on the executive. What did you see that brought
you to the realization that the union was part of the problem, rather
than a body in opposition to management or to capitalism or what
have you?

Petelle:
It was very easy. When you get out of school, and you enter the labour

38

force you're blind because you've never been given any intellectual ammunition to deal with the institutions that you'll be in. You realize quite quickly that unions function as the watchdogs of the system, alerting the society to any labour unrest that arises. There is a difference between the kind of unionism we had in the thirties, and the kind we have now. At one time, unions actually challenged the social system but today it's a question of dividing up the economic pie. If you accept a piece of the pie, you're helping to legitimize the existence of the whole pie. In other words, you're accepting the basic social system that bakes the pie. How did I find this out? It was easy. I was on the negotiating team for two contracts at G.M. and whenever I returned from the negotiations and talked to the guys on the line, I discovered a wide gap between what was being negotiated and what the guys really wanted. The difference was like night and day. The negotiations always centered around problems that the corporation considered manageable.

Johnson:
Well, let's get back to the executive. These people were workers who had been active in the union from the very beginning when the plant was built. What made them less militant?

Petelle:
When you're negotiating with G.M. in Ste-Thérèse, you're not negotiating as a power unto yourselves. The international union is negotiating with the corporation as a whole in Detroit. And they're looking at the general aspects of the problem. It's true that you have local negotiations but it's really quite unimportant because you don't have the power of the big international union to back you up. The local issues remain local issues and you're left on your own to deal with them. What you need with a company like General Motors is negotiating power and it's almost impossible without the help of the international. We saw martyr plants that went on strike for six to eight months to fight for local issues and they got very little because they didn't have the bargaining power of the international behind them. So, knowing that, meaning knowing more than the average worker that you represent, you tend to back off a little on the demands which you have been asked to negotiate. The best thing for a negotiating team would be to have the whole goddamn process out in the open, in a big hall with the company up front, a few union representatives, and the entire membership present. The issues would be resolved very quickly, let me tell you.

Johnson:
Nothing could be hidden and any compromise would have to be made in front of the membership.

Petelle:

That's right, and they would be able to accept or refuse that which was being negotiated, but in our goddamn society we tend to delegate authority and do things behind closed doors.

Johnson:

So you felt that, under the existing framework, your function was to get the best possible package deal for the guys and that was the limit of what you could do.

Petelle:

Well, you always try to do the best but, we're in a society with many frills. Most of the union men that I know really believe that they're doing their best. And I really think that they are doing their best given the present negotiating framework. But they know that if they push too hard in certain areas, they're going to end up on the street looking for a new job. You're caught up in the merry-go-round.

Johnson:

In your own case, Claude, you got into a lot of trouble because you didn't exactly play the game, the way you were supposed to. What happened when you went beyond the established procedures? What was the reaction?

Petelle:

Well, you were reprimanded by the international rep. Let's take, for example, the question of the working language in Québec. It was the demon that affected more people than anything else. It's true that workers who had supervisors that could speak French had few problems but there were sections of the plant with supervisors that couldn't speak a work of French. So we were pushing this issue because many workers were faced with the problem of not knowing what the score was. They couldn't communicate, and in our society being what it is, communication is very important in terms of promotion. The French speaking workers felt that they were being left at the bottom of the heap, because of their language problem.

Johnson:

Well, it wasn't really their problem. It was management's problem. After all, we're living in a French-speaking province. It really wasn't the workers' problem at all. They were made to feel that it was their problem so they felt an even greater resentment.

Petelle:

That's true and even the international union made them feel this way. Most of the top officials in the U.A.W. were English-speaking people from the United States and they didn't want to deal in French either.

They felt we should speak English because they didn't want to take the trouble to learn French and to provide us services in French. We were pushing the French issue very hard and we were eventually told to cool it. I even got into a fight with an international rep, not a fist fight because the international Vice-President stopped me, but if I had got my hands on him, I would have throttled him.

Johnson:
What was the fight about?

Petelle:
Well, he called me a fucking frog and told me I should speak English because I worked for G.M.

Johnson:
Well, that's absurd because when a company like G.M. locates in Germany, the management is expected to speak German.

Petelle:
That's true, but this was the feeling both of the company and the international union, so we were left with a hell of a problem and we had to downplay it.

Johnson:
Because they were still convinced that Québec is a conquered colony and there's a colonized mentality?

Petelle:
Well it is, it is a colonized area we're living in. The only difference is that there's more hypocrisy surrounding the situation than in other colonized areas. And the guy who insulted me knew that and, believe me, it's hard to take. Maybe it's our fault because we're not strong enough as an entity to change that view of things. But again, it's a situation where other problems are created while the real problems are often ignored. The basic problem of labour versus monopoly capital is not confronted because the language problem is so important to individuals, the right to speak their own language, that everything else is camouflaged.

Johnson:
Give me another example of a situation where you felt that you had to go beyond normal procedures.

Petelle:
Well, for instance, I think that unions in our society have a special task. That task is to protect the worker because, after all, the union was created for that reason. And, also to use the union structure to contest this society that we live in. I wanted to use the structure as a rallying

point for radical social change. So I went up to the international President with this idea. To use this structure as a real arm of power for workers. But the international President and the rest felt that it wasn't our job to push or raise shit or question the value of the system. They were telling me that everybody was happy and that's just not true. And they should know but they forget very goddamn fast once they're off the shop floor.

Johnson:
Because they've made it in a way. Much the same as a person who's just been made office manager. They are in a position of authority and prestige and they're no longer concerned about problems affecting "ordinary" rank and file workers.

Petelle:
And they help to maintain this myth that people are incapable of directing their own lives without constant supervision and Godlike figures of authority. They begin to believe that they are better than the people who elected them representatives.

Johnson:
People in this position tend to cash in on their verbal skills. In most cases, workers have become union representatives because of an ability to shoot off their mouths.

Petelle:
It's not only that, Walter. It's a question of wanting to be in that position. Then you develop the skills that will help you remain in that position.

Johnson:
It's your desire to be in that position and what you have to do to achieve that end. Like brownnosing to become boss.

Petelle:
And brownnosing to become international rep. I was offered the job of international rep and I was also offered a foreman's job. But I wouldn't accept either of the jobs because it wasn't really going to do me any good. Money is the least important thing to me. As long as I have food, shelter and clothing, my basic needs are satisfied. And I also felt that workers didn't need any more union reps telling them what to do. What they really needed were people in the same position as they were who knew the way the system operated.

Johnson:
You wanted to affect the consciousness of rank and file workers. Unless there is a real change in the consciousness of workers at the base, nothing that happens will be worthwhile.

Petelle:
I've always believed that first you must know them and then you must unite and then you will win. In French I say, *"Soyons conscience unisons nous et nous vaincrons."* It's difficult but these things must happen before we have any real improvement in the human condition.

Johnson:
Part of the problem is that we've been raised to compete with each other.

Petelle:
Well, just remember the educational system that we went through. You had a first and a last in the class, you had gold stars. Sports are another example. It's one of the worst influences in our society. We're giving children the idea that they always must be winners. Winners of what? A goddamn golden puck, a cheap trophy, you name it. People don't play sports for pleasure, they play to win at all costs and this attitude carries over to our work environment. Every man is a potential competitor. Look at the number of hours devoted to sport on television every week-end. It's not the joy of physical expression that's been shown, it's the pleasure of dominating our fellow men. And being raised and educated towards that type of competition you carry on being competitive with everyone around you.

Johnson:
You would think, though, that in a big industrial enterprise like General Motors, co-operation should be the norm because without a large degree of co-operation the plant just couldn't function. To me, the company creates an artificial kind of competition because the natural tendency in a place like G.M. is to work co-operatively, to help each other. The only barriers to co-operation are these stupid job titles that management have bestowed upon workers through the job classification system. You know, I'm better than the guy next to me because I'm an inspector. That type of thing.

Petelle:
As soon as you give people titles you're asking for trouble. We're living in a very specialized society which is pretty bad.
At one time many people did complete jobs. Now, more and more people must make their living by doing fragmented labour tasks.

Johnson:
But surely that should bring about the necessity for co-operation rather than competition because if one guy is doing part of a job and his mate the other part, they can't accomplish the task unless they are willing to collaborate?

Petelle:
Well, I don't agree with you. I don't think the fragmented work process can really satisfy people. People are dissatisfied with themselves because there is no sense of completion or roundedness in the jobs they are doing. They're not in control of their own lives. They realize that they are only little cogs in a very big wheel, pieces of meat. And they also realize that they can be replaced very goddamn easily. So they feel insecure, even though this society tries very hard to convince people that they're more secure than people have been at any other time in history. People are more insecure because their lives are divided into totally unrelated parts. Family life and work life are separated. Leisure activities are increasingly mechanized and escapist. The tensions of everyday life have multiplied alarmingly.

Johnson:
How can workers change this?

Petelle:
In any process, people have to accept themselves. If you're a man with one leg, and you keep on being dissatisfied because you can't have another leg, you'll be miserable all your life. The same goes for workers. In our society a worker is a kind of cripple because of the social ethos but if people accept themselves as workers, and begin to regard workers as noble people, things will change for the better. And, of course, workers are the most useful people in our society because if everybody was a boss, nothing would get done.

Johnson:
How do you go about developing this sense of worth or usefulness?

Petelle:
Well, we're living under a system which makes it almost impossible for this type of consciousness to develop among workers.

Johnson:
Don't you think that the contradictions of everyday life produce a kind of questioning process which ultimately might result in a change of consciousness. When a person is unsatisfied with himself, he's got to look at the reasons for his dissatisfaction.

Petelle:
Yeah, but the society is capable of handling this dissatisfaction very easily. It responds to a worker's dissatisfaction by offering him a wide array of commodities at the marketplace. If a guy is watching T.V. or playing hockey or driving around on a high powered ski-doo, he forgets about the problems that bother him.

Johnson:
Yeah, but when he goes back to the goddamn job on Monday morning, he knows he must spend the next five days on a shitpile. You were saying that a door screwer at G.M. is going to have a hard time, is going to have to accept a reduction in pay, if he leaves the company for "greener" pastures. Knowing this, he's more willing to accept the crap that's heaved at him daily to make a living. And the goods, the stereos, T.V.'s, and whatnot, offer some compensation for his insecurity. It gives the worker a false sense of security that he wouldn't have otherwise, and that he needs because the job isn't providing him with any feeling of security.

Petelle:
The only security for him is to stay where he is because the society doesn't provide many alternatives. The more fragmented the labour process becomes the more difficult it will be for workers to move and change jobs. In Russia, they don't issue travelling passes so you don't travel. But at least they're frank about it. They tell you directly. But here, we're doing it in a subtle way. We're led to believe that we're free, but we're not. Our movement is becoming more restricted because of specialization. An automobile worker has a choice of maybe three or four cities where he *might* be able to get a job. And the chances of getting a job in these cities is very slim. And worst of all, we're eliminating our ability to communicate with each other. For example, if you're a technician in aerospace technology or miniaturized electronics, you just can't relate or communicate with anybody other than another aerospace technician or electronic technician. Workers don't seem to realize the direction that our capitalist society is leading us. If you have ever read George Orwell's *1984*, you can see why he was a real prophet.

Johnson:
As time goes on, do you think that workers will have even less control of their own destiny than they do now, or will the problems that have been created by specialization and fragmentation bring about a change of consciousness?

Petelle:
My consciousness had changed because of the work environment, and if my consciousness can be changed, then the consciousness of other workers can also change. We're not all blind. We look at life and we discover things about work and life and, hopefully, we don't try to hide what we discover.

Johnson:
Is the automobile industry necessary and worthwhile?

Petelle:

I don't think that we should be building automobiles. I think it's stupidity. The automobile industry has replaced the medieval rack as a means of eliminating people, about 700 people a week in the United States and 300 in Canada. We know that the automobile is the absurdity of late twentieth century life. It's unsafe, it pollutes, it's a useless hunk of metal in five or six years, it consumes our oil and gas, which we will need in future decades for more important uses. Energy should be conserved and not exploited just to satisfy the fantasies of frustrated North Americans. On Sunday, people are out driving everywhere but they don't really see anything. Casesar was right when he said, "Give the people bread and games and they'll be contented." Cars are the modern day equivalent. Workers could run the factories now, but I really question whether it is worthwhile.

Johnson:

We can only bring about real change by ourselves. We can't depend on the State to solve our problems for us. Right now, people in the Liberal government are pushing this concept of industrial democracy, whereby workers would have more control over their work environment. Do you think that this is just another bullshit concept with an illusion of participation, while the private profit system still remains intact? Perhaps, the ultimate rationalization of production, capitalism's "final solution" to the nagging problem of employee dissatisfaction?

Petelle:

Any so-called progressive scheme promoted by the State always brings a smirk to my face. It's absurd when people in government try to "help" the working class. They don't represent our class, therefore any solutions they propose serve their interests and their class. Who knows more about workers and working than workers themselves? It's only the rank and file, the people who are being oppressed at the workplace, who can fundamentally change our society. It can't be changed by people who say they represent the interests of workers when, in reality, they are only using the working class to further their own interests.

Johnson:

This is also the case with many intellectuals who are using workers to further their own ends. There are many intellectuals crouching on the periphery of the trade union movement who give a certain input of ideas and suggestions but they're also using their connections with the working class to advance their academic careers.

Petelle:

You're going to see more and more people using the working class as their stepping stone to further themselves or obtain some kind of power over others.

Johnson:
Or even to get in a position where they don't have to work so hard. In my own case, for example, when I received a grant to write among other things, about conditions in the automobile industry. The government gives me a grant and says "You're free, you can write about what's bugging you." It's an example of how far they'll go to keep people satisfied or at least contented. But my friends back at the factory must continue being miserable.

Petelle:
The Company of Young Canadians is a good example of this sort of thing, or the Local Initiatives Programs or Opportunities for Youth. They are all programs which take the dissenting or contesting forces in our society and canalize them into less disruptive activities. The unions today function in much the same way. Unions often stifle spontaneous rank and file actions by using the grievance procedure. It's deadening.

Johnson:
People are continually being absorbed into the established framework. Dissenters are offered a place in society where their dissent is legitimized and institutionalized. You see this happening all the time, especially with many intellectuals who very often are really frustrated businessmen.

Petelle:
I discovered that at least fifty percent of the people involved with the union were really frustrated foremen or managers. It was really goddamn bad after a certain period as a union representative to see many people were accepting management jobs and management philosophy. And this stems from the fact that our upbringing in this society programmes people for this type of behaviour. We've got to change the basic programming or we'll never change the society. It's as simple as that. Understanding that is simple, but to bring about the change will require patience, education and very hard work.

Working on the
Assembly-line

by Jim Monk

I started work at a truck assembly plant in Windsor in September, 1973 and with several short interruptions was there steadily for over eight months. It took quite a while before I was able to develop a clear picture of everything going on around me. Nobody had to tell me that there was a war being waged on the shop floor. But exactly how that war was being fought, its goals and its forms of struggle, was so subtly obvious that I had been fighting for some time before I became aware of exactly what I was fighting for.

The everyday activity in the truck plant seems to have three major goals which workers are trying to achieve. The first of these is a constant attempt to decrease productivity, lighten our work load, and therefore increase or at least maintain the manpower in the plant. Directly connected to this is the second goal, that of shortening our working day. Finally there is the struggle to improve physical working conditions like how hot it gets, how dirty our work area is, how slippery the floor is, etc.

These three kinds of struggle in particular are marked by the fact that they are directly carried out by the workers as they work. In these cases there is little or no mediation by the union (the UAW). Other struggles, however, seem especially prone to co-option and control by the union; for example, actions to show support for disciplined or discharged workers. The union has also tried to increase manpower in a plant by encouraging us not to work overtime while the others are laid off. By first calling for an overtime ban and then cancelling it, the union has used the overtime issue as a bargaining tool against management. But generally, the struggles to decrease production, shorten the working day, and improve working conditions take place without the intervention or interference of any external organization, union or other.

The slowdown is the most common form of the struggle to decrease production. Deliberately not making production by going

---

Jim Monk works at the Chrysler truck plant in Windsor, Ontario.

into the hole, performing unnecessary motions, requesting a pass to see the nurse, arguing with the foreman as the work goes on down the line is the first defense against speed-up and an offensive tactic as well. This may be done individually but more often small groups of workers co-operate with each other by collectively slowing down. The co-operation is necessary not only because it makes it harder for management to fix the blame on any one individual, but also because this co-operation is necessary to run the production line in the first place.

A variation of the slowdown is to run out of stock and shut the line down for lack of material. Foremen are so busy that they seldom have a chance to keep tabs on how much stock workers have on hand. There is not a thing a foreman can do to us when directly in front of his eyes someone reaches over and pushes the line button and starts yelling at him to get us some more stock or we'll get the general foreman to fire him. Running out of stock usually requires the cooperation of stock chasers and jitney drivers who must arrange to be conveniently busy elsewhere when we begin to run low on something. Often a worker will strike up a conversation with his foreman as a distraction while others hide stock material or quickly use up what little is left.

Sabatoge is very frequent. It tends to be performed more by individual workers than by groups and this is only natural, for the penalty for being caught is immediate firing with almost no chance of being hired by other auto companies. There are two kinds of sabotage. One way is to disrupt the line by putting an obstacle in a link and jamming it. This shuts things down for five minutes to half an hour while the mill-wrights make the repairs. The other method is more common: making deliberate mistakes in your work. When this is done by large numbers of workers the company is forced to shut down all production for several days while the repair department catches up on all the rejects.

In one department I worked in, we decreased production by increasing the space between units on the line. This was the miscellaneous paint department. The men are divided into three categories: loaders, painters and unloaders. The painters generally have the most seniority and the loaders, the least. It is the responsibility of the loaders to put parts such as bumpers, instrument panels, headlight rings and brackets on to the hooks of a conveyor line that carries the parts through the paint booths and drying ovens and back out to the unloaders. Each part is supposed to be put on the line with a set spacing of so many empty hooks separating it from the other parts. For example, instrument panels are loaded with two empty hooks between them. Whenever we can, we load them at a distance of three or four hooks apart. Similar expansions are attempted with other parts and it is a continual game between us and the foremen to see who determines the spacings of the parts. Everyone in the department assists the loaders in this, because naturally the less work the loaders do, the less work everyone else does.

Another practice which is common in most departments is splitting work with a partner. This has also been called doubling up. Instead of both workers working on the line all the time, one partner will cover both jobs for twenty minutes while the other takes a break. By switching back and forth who does the work and who rests, we usually only really work for half a shift, four hours, and just put in time for the other four, playing cards, reading etc. What is significant here is that there is no attempt to hide this splitting of work from the foreman. He is quite aware of it and will not ask you to do something if he knows that your partner is the one working at present. Some older workers are upset by this kind of thing. They are afraid that time study will eventually come into the department and cut the manpower in half. But most of the older workers and all the younger ones seem confident that the struggle they will put up should a manpower cut be attempted will make any such move a futile and disastrous one.

The splitting of work is one example of what I have called the struggle to shorten the working day. It's not precisely what is usually meant when we speak of shortening the working day, but it does show how workers try to give as little time as possible to the company and keep as much time for themselves as they can. This objective appears to be an important factor in the numerous illegal work stoppages experienced by the auto companies in Windsor. When workers in the truck plant walked out on April 1st to protest the firing of the union chairman, the fact that it was a nice day outside was given by many as the real reason they wanted to go, as many couldn't care less what the company did to the union reps. A real shortening of the working day is difficult to achieve, but it is relatively simple for workers to shorten the work week. Absenteeism, calling in sick when you're perfectly healthy and just don't want to work, is so prevalent that often the company has to use relief men to cover absent workers jobs, as there are not enough absentee replacement men to go around. On these days, instead of relief being spread out over the length of the day, the company will shut a whole department or even all production down to give everyone their relief at the same time.

One of the most dramatic forms of workers' struggle is the walkout. There has only been one since I started work, but with summer coming I'm told that they should become a fairly frequent occurrence as truck plant workers refuse to work in excessive heat. Before the April 1st walkout the union had repeatedly told us that walking out only served to gut the union. When the union chairman was fired, our plant union committee promptly decided to call a walkout. The abrupt reversal of policy did not go unnoticed by workers who had attended the union meeting the day before! But word of the walkout was quickly spread throughout the plant and workers discussed whether or not they should go out, with most but not all finally deciding to leave. My work area was in the annex across the street from the main plant and the discussion there centred around the fact that the annex workers wanted to make sure the main plant walked out first before they left. The summer before during the heat walkouts, the annex workers had always left first as they worked in the hottest areas, and several times the main plant workers waited to be sent home rather than walk out themselves. A number of annex workers resented this and waited for some time before walking out on April 1st. In my department everyone wanted to walk out but no one would walk out alone. They didn't feel it was safe to walk out unless they did so as a group, which they finally did after I went out by myself out of impatience to see what was happening at the plant meeting in the local union hall.

This walkout was called by the union, a very rare event and very embarrassing to the local officials. But there was no automatic acceptance of the union's leadership. A sizeable minority of workers did not leave the plant until sent home by the company. Of the workers who did walk out only about half attended the union meeting which we were all supposed to head towards on leaving the plant. The plant chairman is not very popular and it is quite probable we would not have walked out at all if the weather hadn't been so pleasant. Who wants to work on a Monday morning? The meeting was short and totally controlled by the union. We were thanked for our support and asked to co-operate with the new acting plant chairman and follow the union's instructions. The union would take care of the firing over the bargaining table. Not one rank and file worker spoke. In the plant the workers were quick to communicate the plan of the walkout to every department including one two miles away in another building. They succinctly debated the pros and cons of the walk out and then acted. The difference between what happened in the plant and what happened at the union meeting was startling.

The only thing more threatening to management than a walkout is a sit-in. The sit-in I was involved in lasted for 55 minutes, at which point the company gave in to every one of our demands. This kind of success is not always the case and was the result of several favourable conditions, the preparation of which took us several weeks.

The job I was on at the time was called "building tires". What we did was to put tires on to their wheel rims, inflate them and then load the tires on to a conveyor line. The job is generally considered the worst in the plant. Truck tires and rims are heavy and we had to carry the rims from ten to twenty feet to our work area from the stock area. We were constantly bending over and lifting tires with our back muscles. After the tire was fitted over the rim, we had to kick the lock ring into place with the heel of a boot while standing on the other foot. The tires were stored outside and in the winter they were covered with snow which melted when brought indoors, soaking our gloves and clothes as well as making the floor slippery. In addition to melted snow we soaped each tire to make it slip onto its rim and the soapy water on the floor made kicking lock rings a dangerous balancing act. The round pots on which we placed the rims were not welded down and tended to move out from under you when you misplaced your kick.

The time study men had always scheduled three men on tires, each one building two tires every four minutes. This alone made the job exhausting. When I was transferred to the job, the foreman was using six men on tires, pulling three from other jobs about to be phased out. This was supposed to be temporary and we were repeatedly told that the job would soon be reduced back to three men. However the six of us were determined to prevent that from happening. We used every conceivable form of slowdown we could think of to prevent them from making production with six men, let alone three. We tormented our foreman so much that he had a nervous break-down and was removed from our department, and put on the night shift to recuperate. We repeatedly told the general foremen to improve the condition of the tire area. He knew that was his only hope of making production but was unable to get the maintenance department to act.

One day our foreman came rushing past our work area and slipped on the soapy floor. He grabbed a pipe and just missed getting a serious knock on the head. We told him right then to clean up the place by noon or we would refuse to work after lunch. For the rest of the morning we made sure the floor was super slippery by spilling soap all over it whenever there was no foreman around. After lunch we came back and there was no improvement. We started to work anyway, but after five minutes the steward came by and we asked him if we had to work on that floor. He said the law gave us the right not to work in unsafe conditions and that we, not him, would have to determine whether it was unsafe. The union, he said, would back us up no matter what we did, but we had decided our own course of action for ourselves.

So we sat down and watched the line run empty. The foreman came by and ordered us back to work. We ignored him. The general foreman came by and we told him why we weren't working. Before we went back to work we wanted the pots welded to the floor, a new grillwork welded to the floor to give us better traction, the soap washed away and someone to take the snow off the tires before they were brought inside. For half an hour nothing happened. Workers from other parts of the annex came over to our area and we were told that if anyone was disciplined, everyone would sit down in support.

53

The top plant management arrived on the scene after almost an hour had gone by. Our steward told us that they had all been out to lunch at the E.C. (local swank bar-restaurant) and were furious at having to leave right in the middle of the first course. They really had their problems now because two other departments in the main plant decided to hold sit-ins themselves when they heard about ours. They wanted to improve working conditions also. We told the plant production manager about our foreman slipping in the morning and he asked what we wanted changed. We told him and he gave orders to have it done right then and there. When we finally went back to work the whole plant was sent home half an hour later because the combined effect of the three sit-ins made further production that day impossible.

According to the union there have been over 23 illegal work stoppages, mostly walk-outs, but sit-ins as well, this year in this particular company's Windsor plants. To dismiss these as just spontaneous outbursts of outrage is a very superficial out-look to hold. These events are just the more obvious examples of workers' organization. The speed with which they develop, the quickness of collective decision-making demonstrate just how well workers really are organized. The continual frustration of this organization by the union can only lead to further developing of their organization by rank and file workers.

The organization of workers in our plant follows the organization of the production process. The plant is broken down into various departments — chassis, metal shop, trim line, motor line, axle lines, paint, etc. The workers in each department operate as a unit, not only in their work, but in their struggles as well. Within each department there are smaller groupings of workers determined according to the logic of how a truck is put together. On this level the co-operation between workers is intense as four or five workers spend the whole day talking with each other, working together, being hassled together, eating together and fighting together. When a worker has worked in one area for a time he develops a bond with the other members of his group which continues to exist even after he has been transferred to another area of the plant. Thus the members of a group will have contacts in most other departments, as well as the experience of having worked in those departments.

The communication network between workers functions erratically at present, but every now and then it demonstrates a potential that indicates how advanced the struggle has become. Besides the division of the truck plant into the main building and the annex, there are two storage areas, the frame yard at plant 3 and the old foundry now used for stock on Kildare road, which are several miles from the plant. But when we walked out the truck plant workers in those areas left work as well. There is a company phone network which has each department equipped with one or two telephones in all four of the Windsor plants. These phones are for the use of company and union personnel but there is no way to stop workers from using them as well. Several weeks ago a meeting was called of workers in one department in the main plant to take place at lunch at the parking lot. Almost as soon as it was called, workers in my department knew about the meeting and I was asked by several to go to it and report back to them what happened. This news may have come by phone or a jitney driver may have brought the message over in person, but however it travelled, I was able to determine that not fifteen minutes elapsed from the union rep's calling the meeting to my being asked to attend.

I would like to describe my impressions of workers' responses to leaflets from the left and how workers view the union.

The union regularly puts plant bulletins and the union local newspaper into the plant. Like all printed material we get our hands on, almost all workers read these things over carefully. There is little discussion between workers of what they read and union material is rarely taken home. Instead it is left lying around or thrown in the garbage after it is read. The response to leaflets from a group of militants has been slightly different. Leaflets about the 'historic content' and work stoppages in a particular plant were read carefully and then folded up and taken home. I only rarely found one in the garbage or on the floor. The same is true of a leaflet two of us put into the plant the day after the walkout. Once again there was no discussion about the leaflets, but workers did talk about the facts or events mentioned in the leaflets as if they were general knowledge, even when the leaflets were the only source of that information. I can only conclude from this that the leaflets have performed a useful purpose in generalizing knowledge amongst workers. Only the last two militants' leaflets have received disparaging remarks from workers, with many of them thrown away or posted up with uncomplimentary comments scrawled on them.

I think the anti-union stance which is so powerfully stressed in their aggressive, strident language is responsible for a certain amount of polarization, turning off some workers while appealing to others who have become extremely frustrated by their deteriorating situation. Last night, I was rather surprised to hear one worker say that he thought he would be better off without a union the way we've been fucked over by our reps, and then ten minutes later, after reading a leaflet with essentially the same message, say that the guys who wrote it were shit disturbers with nothing constructive to offer.

This brings us to the rather contradictory way in which workers view the union. On the one hand, almost everyone is well aware that the stewards and committeemen exercise a certain amount of control over them, just like a foreman. When a foreman is having a discipline problem he can't immediately resolve, he, not the worker, will call for the steward. The steward will have a friendly talk with the worker and explain why he has to do what he is told. Foremen continually rely on stewards to bail them out of trouble. Because a union rep has no responsibilities to meet production and supervises a much larger part of the plant than the foreman, he has a clearer conception of what's going on and can act as an effective troubleshooter. The meeting in the parking lot, for example, was called by the union to quell a growing movement for a walkout in that department.

Workers in my department constantly comment on how the union works against us. On the other hand, workers often use their union reps and the union as someone would use a lawyer when they get in trouble with the authorities. Workers will reject union leadership of their shopfloor struggle but will insist that the union represent them after a struggle has resulted in some discipline. Increasingly the workers are relegating the union to just that kind of role, retaining the union as a legal representative in collective bargaining and discipline procedures, while the rank and file directs the struggle against the company themselves.

This dual perspective on the role of unions by workers, as well as the fact of the highly advanced organization of workers in their autonomous struggle, has certain implications for the form and style, as well as the content, of any leaflets or papers the left may put into a plant. Any form of nagging, pushing revolution, or telling the workers to get organized is useless and only serves to irritate workers. Any comment about the union should be careful to separate those functions workers still want the union to fulfill and those functions which work against workers. Nothing written should ever imply that workers expect the union to lead them in their struggles. There is no use hammering away at the point that the union is not fighting to improve our working conditions when the last thing workers (excluding trade unionists of course) want is interference from the union. If a leaflet is going to have agitational statements and emotionally charged sentiments, these should be quotes from rank and filers which are representative of the comments currently being made by large numbers of the rank and file, and explicitly presented as quotes; otherwise an impression is given that a few enlightened workers or leftists are trying to awaken their fellow workers to a situation that only a few correctly perceive. Even though I am sure that this impression is not intended, workers have it and quite rightly resent it.

Working in a Printing Shop

interview with Ron Sigler

Johnson:
Ron, what kind of shop were you working in?

Sigler:
It's one of the many small print shops that are so common in Montreal.
We had about fourteen employees in the production department and
a couple of people in the office. We did the full range of printing
from the photographing of the initial copy down to the binding in the
end. There were three of us in the preparation department which is
where we take the original copy, sometimes do some artwork on it,
and then make the final plates that go to the printing presses. It goes
to the press room where most of the production staff work, about six
or seven people. There are six or seven different size presses from small
and multilith to about forty inch size. From there the copy went to the
bindery, where there were two very underpaid women doing a lot more
work than they should have been doing.

Johnson:
What were you doing?

Sigler:
I was working in the preparation department. In this particular shop
the trade was not as divided as it is in many other shops. I was doing
camera work, stripping of the film, and then final plate making, blue-
prints, and other kinds of proofs to show the customer exactly what
they were going to get before it went on the press.

Ron Sigler is an apprentice printer and lives and works in Montréal.

Johnson:
Is the work interesting?

Sigler:
It can be quite satisfying because you have a fair amount of control
over what you do and what the final product looks like.

Ron Sigler is an apprentice printer and lives and works in Montréal.

Johnson:
How did you relate to the bosses? Did you have much autonomy?

Sigler:
We were quite well off in that respect. The bosses don't really know the trade so they have to take the word of the workers around that things are going right. If we listened to the bosses, nothing would ever work out. And they realized that as long as they would leave us alone, things would work smoothly.

Johnson:
Do you feel that the shop could have functioned without any kind of supervision?

Sigler:
We did quite well without supervision most of the time. The only time we had any real problems was when there were contradictory instructions. As a matter of fact, one of the fellows from my department was fired three or four times because he told the boss off in very graphic terms, about what he thought of his instructions. Each time he was fired he was re-hired a couple of days later by one of the other bosses who realized that, of course, he was right all the time and didn't want to let a good man go.

Johnson:
He felt that he was somewhat indispensable, contrary to most businesses or organizations where a guy is just another piece of meat?

Sigler:
Exactly. In the printing trade, there are not that many skilled people around and the work is really quite complicated when you get down to it, even though it doesn't necessarily seem so on the surface.

Johnson:
Do you think that people in this line of work feel any alienation? In many industries, people have so little control over their jobs that there is a kind of personal estrangement. Do you think this exists in the printing industry?

Sigler:
Well, I think there is some of that in every industry, but I don't think that printing is one of the worst. I guess it varies, depending on the type of work you are doing within the industry. In my trade, pre-plate work, the job is complicated enough to keep your mind active for the period of time that you are there. It keeps you active in a mental way so you don't feel that you're just working mechanically. In that sense it is, perhaps, not as alienating as other kinds of industry.

Johnson:
Are there any types of printing which are becoming more fragmented and routinized?

Sigler:
Yes, that's definitely happening as things become increasingly mechanized, and larger and more complicated machinery does more of the work that was previously left to judgement and human touch. In the film work, for example, what used to be done in the past by hand development and a trade, which would require variables that you had control over, is now done in automatic processors. Now you just get your exposures and your times down right, feed your film in, and you get the identical product all the time. Before you had a certain amount of craftsman's pride in it, but now it's just purely mechanical.

Johnson:
Do you think that there has been any conscious effort by management or experts in this area to de-skill printing jobs because it makes employees more dispensable?

Sigler:
Sure. Whenever the volume of work will justify it economically, the large machinery will do the work of several men. With the large machinery, one man can do the work that previously required four men to do by hand.

Johnson:
So there's more of a conscious effort to make the work more efficient rather than to de-skill the job?

Sigler:
Oh, there's no question about it. The trend today is towards more machinery and fewer employees and, of course, fewer skilled workers. The trend is also toward employees who are trained to operate one particular machine as opposed to workers who know the trade in depth. This way, a person is at the mercy of the company because unless he can find a job somewhere else with the identical machine, he really doesn't know enough to get by.

Johnson:
So you think that the era of the well rounded craftsman is coming to an end as far as printing is concerned?

Sigler:
Not yet. I think there is a long way to go, but that is the trend. The union is fighting certain kinds of mechanization, and remember that even the modern machinery does require a certain amount of skill to operate. But the kind of craft we used to have in the old days, when

things were really done in a personal way, is gone. And, of course, the new machinery reduces the number of people needed in the trade. There are machines now that will print, fold, bind and cut things that previously were operations performed by whole groups of people in various trades. Now two or three people man each section of a machine and they watch over a particular aspect of the machine's function. And the work is completely alienating because you are just a part of the machine essentially, and what goes in as paper and plates on one end comes out as printed books on the other. In that kind of situation there is just not too much to relate to really.

Johnson:
What caused the strike at your shop?

Sigler:
Working conditions weren't bad really. The main problem was that some of the older men wanted a little more job security. They had seen people fired for no real reason other than a misunderstanding with the boss. Also, the wages varied considerably. There were people in the shop who were getting the full union wage. There was even one guy who was getting overscale but he was a good friend of the boss so that was to be expected. But myself as an apprentice, I was getting about half of what I should have been getting in a union shop. I was working very hard for about three dollars an hour. When the shop sold my work to the customer, they were charging $17.50 an hour, so you can see the discrepancy. The women in the bindery department were also hit very hard. Even in a union shop, the bindery workers' wages are not that good.

Johnson:
What goes on in the bindery department?

Sigler:
People in the bindery department work smaller machinery and do hand binding and stitching.

Johnson:
Is this type of work as complicated as the work in other departments?

Sigler:
It's not as complicated and doesn't take as long to learn, but it still takes a lot out of you. It's hard work. You put in a very hard day. And the women were making under three dollars an hour. And it's still skilled work, regardless of whether or not it takes a person ten years to learn it. We, as a group, considered their wage rates totally unacceptable. And they were also the kind of women who were very shy and some-what unwilling to confront the very tough type of characters of the bosses.

Johnson:
Tough in what way?

Sigler:
There were two of them, two brothers who owned the shop. One of them was a playboy type who would throw his money around, live high and regard anyone around him as a tool for whatever purpose he could use them. This applied especially to women who he didn't quite regard as human beings.

Johnson:
Sexist.

Sigler:
Yes, sexist and racist I might say.

Johnson:
So you felt that the women in the shop were really getting the short end of the stick?

Sigler:
That's for damn sure. Their wages were at poverty level.

Johnson:
Were they resistant to organizing efforts? Perhaps too shy to assert themselves?

Sigler:
They were too shy to deal with their problems as individuals, but they were not resistant to organizing efforts. As a matter of fact, they were as tough as anyone could be when it came to picket duty during the strike. For several months leading up to the strike the union office had negotiated with the bosses trying to establish a contract because most of the shop was already certified by the Quebec Government as being officially organized by the Graphic Arts International Union. The negotiations headed absolutely nowhere so we went to a government conciliator but the bosses completely refused to meet with the conciliator. They made a few token gestures but they would not agree to have a union in the shop. The bosses didn't want to have anyone interfere with their holy management prerogatives. They had a very old fashioned view that all unions were communist and devil inspired and were out to castrate or destroy them. That is the way they related to these things. I had long talks with one of the bosses, who really didn't seem to understand what the whole thing was about. This guy was so much of a macho individualist that he was personally determined to crush the union at all costs and make an example to all the owners of the small print shops in Montreal. He wanted to show people that the union could be beaten and if, in fact, he had to bankrupt his company

he would do it. And, frankly, I believe that he would have done just that.

Johnson:
Was he very sophisticated politically in a reactionary sort of way, or was he just a defender of the *status quo?*

Sigler:
He was a defender of the *status quo,* but he was politically ignorant. He wasn't even so much as an aware right-wing capitalist.

Johnson:
He just felt that he was boss and that was the natural order of things so the union be damned?

Sigler:
I think that that was the limit of his understanding. He felt that society was divided into those who rule and those who are meant to be used by those who rule.

Johnson:
How, then, did the strike come about?

Sigler:
After the negotiations proved totally fruitless, we realized that we had two choices. Either find new jobs or make an attempt to force the bosses into some kind of settlement. So, when the legal time came, after sixty days of conciliation, we had a strike vote at the union local and voted to go out, and we did. But there were five people in the shop who never supported the union. Let me backtrack a little bit. There were two people of that five that actually did sign union cards, that came to the union meetings, and then, on the day of the strike vote, said not only were they against the strike but they were going to cross the picket line. They were pretty nervy to say that in the union office but they did it all the same. As it turned out, they were true to their word. I imagine they had a nice little gift from the boss for their traitorous actions.

Johnson:
You mean their allegiance had been bought?

Sigler:
Yes.

Johnson:
By an increase in pay or by a lump sum payment?

Sigler:
Probably an increase in pay and possibly a lump sum gift. But mostly by fast talk and ideology. By telling them that they weren't really

workers. They weren't really low down French types who were meant to be stepped on and exploited. The boss tried to make them believe that they were something special, even friends of his. The thing is, you see, that in a small shop, people do develop close personal relationships with their employers and that is what, in a way, crippled us in the long run. One of the bosses was a real smooth talker so by telling some of the workers, you know, "You're my friend, come up for the weekend to my country cottage, come fishing with me, I'll buy you a drink, boys". That's really all it takes for some people.

Johnson:
Did you know the wage rates for the other workers in the shop?

Sigler:
Pretty much.

Johnson:
You knew, then, who was getting more money and for what reason?

Sigler:
Exactly. It's hard, in a small shop, to keep those things secret and, besides, most of us weren't interested in keeping those things secret anyway.

Johnson:
How many people in the shop decided to scab when you went on strike?

Sigler:
Eight people went out and five guys scabbed.

Johnson:
Was there much hostility between the two groups?

Sigler:
There was a great deal of hostility and it could have become a very violent situation if there weren't a lot of things restraining people on both sides — ultimately the law. Both sides realized that if it ever came to violence we would not stop at anything.

Johnson:
Did the police actually protect the workers who wanted to get into the shop?

Sigler:
For the first few days they kept an eye on scabs who crossed the picket line, but eventually they realized that there wasn't much happening. They knew that we weren't about to attack anybody physically.

Johnson:
Do you think that the police were sympathetic?

Sigler:
They never expressed much sympathy for the scabs but they did have a certain sympathy for the boss. They felt he had a right to keep his shop open if he could. They would say to us, "After all, boys, it's the law."

Johnson:
How did the bosses manage to keep the shop going with only five production workers?

Sigler:
It wasn't easy. It took a long time before he was able to get back to any kind of normal production. But he was willing to incur great losses in order to prove his point and keep his shop free of unionism. Much of the work was sent to outside shops so he was basically functioning on a non-profit basis but, nevertheless, keeping his customers supplied. Then again, what could be done in his own shop was still done there. They had one person in the preparation department who handled camera work, stripping and plates on a simple level. So they could keep that running. They also had one guy for the large press, another on the small press, and yet another for the letterpress. They had no one in the bindery at first, but it didn't take long to find a couple of people, friends and relatives of the scabs, to fill in the remaining jobs. I imagine that they were paid quite well to fill these jobs.

Johnson:
This must have had a bad effect psychologically, on the guys picketing.

Sigler:
Yeah, sure, it had to. After all, here we were standing outside watching people cross the line and knowing that we really could do nothing about it, knowing that the law had everything stacked on the bosses' side. All they had to do was find somebody who was willing to cross the picket line and they were okay. And there was really nothing we could do, within the law.

Johnson:
And you didn't believe in any other type of action.

Sigler:
Sure we did! We believed in anything that would work.

Johnson:
What about intimidation?

Sigler:
We tried and it worked to a certain extent. They made a lot of mistakes because they were scared on the inside. A lot of good people went into the garbage can during this strike. But, ultimately, either we were going to make good on our threats or we wouldn't be taken seriously. And when it came down to it, the situation never seemed desperate enough to justify actual physical violence, even though, at times, that's what we wanted to do. We wanted to physically demonstrate to the scabs the error of their ways.

Johnson:
Were you getting any money while you were on strike?

Sigler:
That's one thing we really were thankful for. The union had a rich strike fund.

Johnson:
The International?

Sigler:
It is the Graphic Arts International Union. The union came into being through a merger of the lithographers, photoengravers, and then the bookbinders. So it's approaching industrial unionism in its structures.

Johnson:
They were giving you financial support even though you had not yet been certified as a local?

Sigler:
Once we had taken out our cards and had been initiated we were *bona fide* members entitled to full strike pay, even though we had not paid more than five dollars a head to the union up until that time. We were receiving about sixty-five dollars a week from the International office in Washington and another forty-five dollars from the Montreal local. So we were receiving about $110.00 per week.

Johnson:
So it wasn't for lack of financial support that the scabs decided to work. If they had decided to support the strike and picket, they would have received the same benefits as everyone else.

Sigler:
Exactly. Some of them, however, were just not willing to go down from $200 a week to $110.

Johnson:
Why? Because of debts and payments to meet?

Sigler:
Well, some of them told us, point blank, that they wouldn't be able to get by on $110 a week. They were not union people, you see. If someone had, however, offered them $300 a week to go on strike, they would have been very happy to comply. Money came before ideology, as it usually does.

Johnson:
As the strike wore on, how were the interpersonal relations among the people who picketed?

Sigler:
They became tighter all the time. We became very close friends in fact. In that way, none of us had any regrets, even when the strike was lost and even though we spent a lot of time, cold weather and hot, on the picket line. After all, we tried to maintain a ten to twelve hour picket line, and with only eight people, that can be quite tough when the weather gets either very hot or very cold. But we became very close. We had time to talk and analyse what was happening, analyse the people on the inside and, most important, analyse our own motives and feelings. In many ways, it was good for us psychologically.

Johnson:
Did this feeling of fellowship continue for the duration of the strike?

Sigler:
It did continue and it got better all the time. We never had any bad interpersonal problems at all, which, to some people, might seem quite unusual. Everyone put in his shifts on the line, everyone got holidays when we decided it was time that the person needed a rest. Things worked purely by consent.

Johnson:
What made you decide to give up the strike?

Sigler:
It was mid winter and we had already been out for close to five months. We knew that the shop was building itself into a stronger position all the time. Slowly, they had been finding people to man the presses. They were getting their paper and supplies across the picket line. Hell, they would come in the middle of the night if they had to and there was no way we could maintain a twenty-four hour picket line. Also, the support from within the local wasn't as strong as it could have been. Sure, we had money but it takes much more than money to win a strike. It takes a lot of people coming down to your picket line and showing their ugly faces to the scabs. And maybe it's necessary to break a few laws every now and then.

Johnson:
This was not the type of strike, then, that can be won simply by picketing?

Sigler:
No way. There is a chance if everybody goes off the job, but in our situation that wasn't the case. Once the work force is divided, it takes more than legal means, because the laws are stacked in favour of the employers.

Johnson:
What advice would you give to other groups undertaking the same kind of strike?

Sigler:
I would say, don't do anything unless you have really got solid backing or, if you do, don't expect that you're going to have your job back. Take it as a gamble and a risk. Take it as an experience, but be prepared to lose your job. In our case, we had a union that was also willing to find work for us, and actually could do it most of the time. As a matter of fact, some of the guys were working part time during the strike and still putting in their picket duty. In other ways though, the union local let us down badly. What we needed desperately, more than anything else, was a physical show of force. We needed people on the picket line at crucial hours like eight o'clock in the morning and four in the afternoon. Also, because we had to split our picket duty, there was never more than three or four people in front of the shop. There's no way four people are very intimidating. Unless people agree with your position, you represent no threat. We needed a show of force but, in fact, there was only one person in the entire local who had the initiative to organize people to come down and help us. And this was a guy who was working swing shifts and could only get to us so often, but he did whatever he possibly could. Had we had a dozen more like him, we would have had a very good chance. He would bring maybe twenty or thirty guys down, stand in front of the shop doors, and glare out into the streets. Nobody would cross the picket line when these guys were around. They didn't have to make threats or carry chains. A few big guys in front of the door and everything was fine. You have to make people afraid to cross the picket. One way or another, intimidation is absolutely essential.

Johnson:
Do you think, perhaps, that the strike was undercut by your local?

Sigler:
In a way. I think there was also a division within the executive of the local. There were one or two guys who were willing to put quite an

effort into settling the strike favourably. And then there were one or two others who didn't give a damn.

Johnson:
As far as they were concerned, the dues that could be received from this shop were not substantial enough to warrant their full support in terms of manpower?

Sigler:
The dues would never pay off the amount they had spent on strike funds, but they were also very cowardly. Some of them said they didn't want to break the law and get a bad reputation with the other employers.

Johnson:
So there was an ideological division within the local as well?

Sigler:
Within the union local there was definitely an ideological division. There was one guy, a lefty type, who really did have a certain sympathy for people involved in these situations. There was another guy, the bigshot type, who felt that his position was very secure and he avoided risks at all costs. He got along very well with the employers, drinking and playing golf with them. The bureaucratic type. Very fat and comfortable. He didn't want to make enemies or do anything to threaten his position. Not for the sake of the workers anyway.

Johnson:
Did any of the other unions in Québec, that have a reputation for militancy, come to your assistance in any way?

Sigler:
Well, we mistakenly felt that our local was going to appeal to higher bodies and try to get some support, but it never worked out that way. Most of the time, nobody knew about our situation.

Johnson:
Was there any publicity in the mass circulation liberal dailies?

Sigler:
Well, the only publicity we ever had was when my wife and I got married and we had a party on the picket line. It made all the newspapers as a human interest story, but that type of thing is quickly forgotten.

Johnson:
So you think that the press is totally useless in reporting on a struggle unless something sensational happens?

Sigler:
Violent or sensationalist. Had we thrown a bomb into the shop, everyone would have known about us immediately. We may have even had
a support committee to get us out of jail. People working very hard
at raising our bail. To avoid that type of thing from happening is a
different story though. For example, we tried to get in touch with student
councils at universities, to see if we could get any kind of support.
As a matter of fact, one of the universities was doing printing at our
shop during the strike. This was a situation where you would call the
student council and say, "Can you at least call your purchasing department and see if they will lay off for the duration of the strike and get
the printing done someplace else and print with a union label?" They
would say, "No, we're not interested. We don't want to have anything
to do with these affairs. Goodbye, sir." So much for the well ballyhooed
campus radicalism.

Johnson:
Do you think a print shop could be run in a better way, other than the
present profit-loss system?

Sigler:
Well, there's no doubt in my mind that all of society could be organized
in a more rational and human way than it is now.

Johnson:
Is it possible, within the shell of the society as it exists today, to run
a print shop co-operatively, without undue concern for profit?

Sigler:
Is it possible, in other words, to humanize the work process within
the present society? Impossible. There's just no way, unless we totally
revamp our morality, our way of living with each other and our view of
each other, as human beings. Whether you're just somebody to be used
or whether you're a fellow worker and a friend.

Johnson:
What about piecemeal or ameliorative reforms? Do you think that
reforms advance the position of the ordinary worker or do they just
tighten the noose?

Sigler:
I think that they can do both things at the same time. There are certain
legal reforms that can make it easier for you to organize small shops
or even large shops and hold their certification, perhaps have a little
bit more to bargain with, but, ultimately, even with a union shop, you
haven't solved your problems. All you've done is put yourself in a new
position on the chess board. You've still got to play the game by the

same old rules. Sure, you can make some changes, but you're still faced with the same job and the same boss.

Johnson:
So you don't think that enlarging an employee's participation in a company is going to work to his advantage while the private profit system still exists?

Sigler:
You're talking about a kind of industrial democracy within capitalism. In a certain way, it can be more satisfying, because you feel that you are more creative in the work that you do and there is less of a mechanical aspect to your day-to-day existence. But, ultimately, all you're doing is working harder to make their enterprise run more smoothly and, as you said, tighten the noose around your own neck.

Johnson:
In your opinion, would workers be willing to accept a management oriented kind of industrial democracy or co-management?

Sigler:
I think there would be two or three frames of mind on that. First of all, it would get a lot of ugly foremen off your back. There are many people who would definitely like to part company with their foreman. But, then again, there are a lot of people who would not want to take the extra responsibility for the same amount of pay. Why take the foreman's job and not get paid for it. You might as well go on the way you have been. You just go on performing your mechanical task and go home and have nothing to worry about or be concerned about.

Johnson:
Lately, a certain Liberal cabinet minister has bandied about this concept of industrial democracy. Is this just another Liberal palliative that doesn't really alter the conditions of work fundamentally and thus, from your point of view, is not satisfying?

Sigler:
Well, as far as government officials using this terminology, it's just a cheap trick. They have no intention of implementing even a fraction of what they are talking about. It's rhetoric. Bryce Mackasey, for instance, talks about industrial democracy while crushing the union. If that isn't giving with one hand, and taking away with the other, I don't know what is.

Johnson:
In your opinion, his outburst was just another in a long line of rhetorical statements?

Sigler:
Well, governments everywhere make rhetorical statements telling you how you live in the most perfect of all worlds and how everywhere outside our borders, things are horrible and chaotic, and everybody is eating their children. Sure they don't mean anything they say. They couldn't possibly, because the people really running the show have money and they'll never willingly relinquish any of their prerogatives. I don't believe that the government means anything when it throws around phrases like "industrial democracy". I think people are living in the clouds if they really expect anything from the State and I don't necessarily mean the Liberal party, or the Canadian government in particular. The Red Chinese government talks about being a workers' government but, in fact, they just sent 10,000 troops into one Chinese province to put the workers down. I don't think that anybody in power can be trusted with sharing that power. It's like a heroin addict. You don't go over to a heroin addict and ask him for a share of his dope. He's just not going to give it to you.

Johnson:
Are workers struggling as much against authoritarianism as anything else?

Sigler:
Yeah, even back in our wee little strike, that's essentially what it was, because the boss was fighting, not so much against giving the workers a higher salary, but against giving them a share in the ultimate power, the running of the show. He wanted to have control over the money and the day-to-day operating in its entirety and, he felt, deep down in his guts, that any attempt to organize the people in the shop into a collective bargaining unit in order to deal with him, was ultimately going to threaten his power. And, as far as that goes, he was right.

Johnson:
He wanted to remain powerful. This is how he got his rocks off.

Sigler:
That's exactly what he did.

Johnson:
How did the strike affect you personally? Did it radicalize you more than before, or did it just confirm what you had always believed?

Sigler:
It confirmed what I had believed for a long time, but it's something else to see things in practice, and in some ways, it's a little more depressing, because you realize how easy it is to be beaten. But, at the same time, it's good to see how solidarity grows between people who didn't know each other very well, and didn't get along that well previously. As

soon as there is something worth struggling for, there is this bond which immediately seems to form. People are helping each other out, taking responsibility, going out of their way for everybody else. The spirit on the line was so good that it was a pleasure to go down to the picket line every morning. You knew that nothing was going to happen, that you weren't going to get anywhere, that you were going to stand around in the sun or cold for hours on end and watch people cross your line. And still it wasn't so bad, because you could relate to the people you were with, and you were building human bonds. And you knew that if you could apply those human bonds to the work situation, the work wouldn't be quite as horrible as we had always known it to be in the past. If we could arrange things in our own way, we wouldn't need bosses. This, actually, seemed to be understood by everybody on the picket line. We would be sitting in the tavern talking about how well things would be in the shop, if we could just get rid of the foreman and the boss. We would discuss various ways the shop would be run and, after a while it became patently clear that we were the only ones who mattered, that if we ran the place ourselves, we would make work into a living and enjoyable experience. We wouldn't kill ourselves, or poison ourselves with fumes and chemicals. We would look out for each other as human beings. Life would be a lot better than it is now. But we also knew that, union or no union, it wasn't going to come about that way. Not under the present system of things anyway. We knew that, even if we did have our victory, we would be going back into the same situation we had come out of. A little bit stronger and wiser perhaps, but still prisoners of a sort. We all knew that there were better ways to live.

Johnson:
Did this feeling of solidarity among the strikers diminish after the strike was broken?

Sigler:
Somewhat. We all had to get away from each other after awhile too, after so much enforced company. Also, the feeling of failure is quite tough to handle. You just have to get away from everything for awhile.

Johnson:
Ron, how did people react to your picket line? In our society, a picket line seems to produce mixed emotions in many people.

Sigler:
It was really varied. We had people from one company, for instance, who would refuse to cross our line, who would be very friendly towards us. But in cases like that, the company would send another driver down, and he would just spit on the ground and drive past us. Generally, the reactions were not as good as I had expected. I had believed that a lot more people respected a picket line than really do. Taxi drivers,

for example. We hear a lot about militant taxi drivers, and the problems that they have. If anybody knows what a struggle means, it's these guys, but our shop had a taxi company that was willing to come by regularly and take orders from the bosses. There were a few drivers who would not come, but there were dozens that would not think twice about taking packages over to the company, or bringing stock over and delivering it. They kept saying, "We don't work here, we're not printing stuff, it doesn't affect us. Why should we ruin our business?" You wouldn't believe the excuses people dream up to rationalize crossing a picket line. People will tell you that there isn't a picket line. One guy told us he was just going into the shop to speak to his brother and, in fact, there never was a union in the shop, and therefore there is no union in the shop, therefore there is no picket line. So, in fact, I'm not crossing a picket line, so what are you guys standing in the street for anyway?

Johnson:
Did some people look down on you for being on a picket line?

Sigler:
Some did, but most people just took the attitude that's bred and drummed into us every day, that your affairs are not my affairs, your business is not my business, and if you guys have a dispute with your boss, fine. There's nothing we can do about it. After all, we're not coming here looking for a job. This is what people would say.

Johnson:
Was there any animosity because you were acting as a group? Many people in our society seem to fear situations where a group of people unites in opposition to authority.

Sigler:
People are definitely afraid of this type of thing. They don't really understand what it is all about. I had assumed that there was a wider understanding in society of what a picket line is, and what a strike represented, but, in fact, I don't think that is so. There was, however, a certain minority, I don't know what the percentage was, who clearly understood the problems and never crossed the picket line.

Johnson:
Are there many small shops of this nature in Montreal, unorganized or lacking union certification?

Sigler:
There are hundreds of small shops. Most of the industry in Québec and Montréal, in particular, is small industry. These shops are either unorganized or poorly organized. A shop might be organized, but that organization does nothing for you.

Johnson:
What are the working conditions in most of these shops like?

Sigler:
I've been in places where you are afraid to walk on the floor because you think you might fall through the floor to the shop below. Or, in other situations, you're afraid that at any moment the machine you are operating is going to kill you. But there are other shops, like the one I worked for, where things are clean, machines are more or less well taken care of and working conditions are fairly good *per se*. It varies drastically from shop to shop. Some shops are horrendous. Some are so horrible that it is beyond belief how anyone can work there.

Johnson:
Have you worked in any of these shops?

Sigler:
Oh yeah. I was in one place like that for about a week and a half. I couldn't last much longer than that. This place had metal sheeting on the floor, which was supposed to protect God knows what, but, in fact, it was never anchored down and was warped, twisting upwards, so you had to walk like a mountain goat to get from one part of the shop to the other — otherwise, you would kill yourself on this thing. There was also machinery which had not been repaired for twenty, maybe thirty years, not to mention the total lack of ventilation in the place, where chemicals were being used, or where there were high concentrations of ozone, which is extremely dangerous.

Johnson:
So over a period of time, a man working in these shops might subject himself to serious illness?

Sigler:
Definitely. Apart from taking the risk of breaking your leg, just from moving around, there were also fork lift trucks in poor condition spilling oil all over the place. And when you get oil slicks on these metal floors, you can expect a one way ticket to the hospital.

Johnson:
You mentioned fumes in poorly ventilated shops. This must have a deteriorative effect over a period of one or two years.

Sigler:
As far as I'm concerned, they have a deteriorative effect over a period of one or two weeks. Ozone, especially, seems to affect me a little more than it affects other people. I can feel sick after a day or two working in a place where the ozone is not properly ventilated and we use a lot of things, electronic carbon arcs, for example, that give off a great amount

75

of ozone. Hell, you can even see it in the air. It takes very good ventilation to avoid any injurious effects. There are places with enclosed dark rooms, plate making machinery in the dark, with no ventilation whatsoever. It's inconceivable that people work that way, but they do, right now. One guy I know, worked for five years under those conditions.

Johnson:
So, obviously, his health was affected.

Sigler:
Certainly. Under those conditions, whose health wouldn't be affected? And there are other chemicals used on the presses and the platemaking which people could be very sensitive to. And even if you're not particularly sensitive to them, they could, over a period of time, build up in your system and cause serious illness. The chemicals used to develop plates are very volatile and a small amount can often make you physically sick. I don't really know what the cumulative effect over a period of years is, but the labels on the chemicals say, "Do Not Breathe the Fumes". That's a good joke, isn't it? There is no way to work with them and not breathe the goddamn fumes.

Johnson:
Do you think conditions in the small shops could be improved, if they organized on a mass scale?

Sigler:
It would probably be a hell of a lot better than it is now. As it is now, the government is not interested in enforcing any kind of health standard. Even if they were somewhat interested, most of the effects of the various chemicals are not really well known. It's only when people start dying like flies that anybody is interested in taking a look at the problem. Workers very often know when something is affecting them badly, even if they don't exactly know what it is. And if there was a large and powerful enough organization that could check things out, find out what was causing the problems, and turn the screws on the employer and threaten him with poor productivity, at least, if he wasn't going to remedy the situation, then there would be a good chance of improving conditions. A strike is not necessarily the best way to solve problems. Even in our own case, we might have been better off, had we stayed in the shop and made things difficult for the boss. It also guarantees your salary. I know a lot of young workers interested in a more radical unionism. The idea of class, them and us, is becoming important to many. Interesting enough the notion of the bosses and the State as being one and the same enemy is widespread. But the traditional union structures are in the way. We need something like the Wobblies.

Assembly-line
merry-go-round

by Walter Johnson

Automobile workers seldom fit the stereotyped image which the media has created. The belief that autoworkers are mindless robots, incapable of anything but the simplest repetitive tasks, is widespread. The image has been popularized by the type of adjectives used to describe assembly work, words like routine, monotonous, robot-like, mechanical, numbing, soul-destroying. The adjectives are appropriate but people should not assume that since the work is dull and mindless the men and women who perform the functions must also be the same. The automobile industry attracts many interesting, offbeat characters who do not expect to remain for more than a few years. The lure is a high starting salary without the intense involvement and commitment which many "responsible" jobs demand. Some men envisage owning a small business or farm. Others invest in bonds or securities hoping eventually to buy themselves out of the work force. Less enterprising types see the big money as an easy way to obtain all the material possessions which our society values so highly. Good pensions, medical care, and disability insurance attract the security conscious; long term disadvantages of assembly work are ignored or dismissed in favour of the immediate benefits. The expectations of many workers seem justified in the initial few months. The work is tedious but a growing bank account and increased purchasing power usually compensate for any feeling of trepidation. Autoworkers' pay-cheques seem enormous to friends who are serving trade apprenticeships or working in offices for a pittance.

However, individual ambitions and schemes are usually cast aside for the immediate satisfactions of coloured television sets, stereos, furniture, and expensive vacation trips. The weekly pay-cheque, which once seemed quite substantial, dwindles to the extent where "making ends meet" becomes a major chore. More adventurous personal goals

---

Walter Johnson worked for many years at the General Motors plant in Ste. Thérèse, Québec. He is an editor of the journal, OUR GENERATION.

soon become impossible as the relentless pressure to balance the family budget increases. Job dissatisfaction increases with the knowledge that old friends are now earning good salaries in more interesting lines of work. Some attempts are made to change jobs but the effort is often futile. Interesting jobs usually pay poorly at the beginning and the worker's weekly expenses can't be met with the type of wage reduction involved. Other high-paying jobs are often as dull as assembly work. Satisfying labour jobs like construction work, lumbering, and cargo handling are seldom available due to high seasonal unemployment or relocation difficulties. To the unskilled operative there are few alternatives to the automobile factory.

As the frustrations mount the disadvantages of auto-industry work become increasingly apparent. In most plants loud buzzers or bells are used to signify starting times, breaks, lunch periods, warnings to return to work station, and quitting times. It is a system which closely resembles prison techniques. Break periods are usually on a rotational basis with absurd time allotments (e.g., twelve, eighteen, or twenty-three minutes in duration). Lunch periods bring crowded line-ups in the cafeteria where men often waste half of their time waiting to be served soupkitchen style. Emergency relief, during work time, for excretory functions is often denied, sometimes leading to ludicrous situations. One employee who was refused such relief protested by defecating at his work station. He was never denied emergency relief again. Employees are required to carry an identification badge, at all times, indicating their department number and name. Failure to display the badge can result in verbal reprimands or other "disciplinary action". Before entering the plant the employee must always show the badge to guards at the plant gate or entrance point. Should the worker forget the badge he is often treated as an errant schoolchild who would "forget his head if it wasn't screwed on". The same attitude applies to absenteeism where a doctor's note is required to "prove" that the employee was actually sick. Some doctors gladly participate in the charade charging ten dollars for a phony sick note.

In some plants soft drink and sandwich machines are restricted to the cafeteria area and workers are prohibited from eating or drinking at their work station. On the job snacks involve a cat and mouse game as workers hide sandwiches or drinks hoping to sneak a bite when supervision isn't around. The automobile industry, particularly General Motors, places tardiness in the same league as original sin. Workers, with no exceptions, who arrive a few minutes late are docked pay as a punitive measure.

Autoworkers cannot refuse scheduled overtime. A nine hour day is not uncommon when sales and production increase. If an employee refuses the overtime he may be subjected to "disciplinary action". It is disheartening to realize that in a society where the thirty-five hour week is considered normal some men will actually be penalized for not working forty-five. Even more disturbing is the knowledge that many unemployed men cannot get ten hours of decent paying work per week. It is a tragic and totally unnecessary waste of human resources.

The puritanism of the automobile industry is in marked contrast to the general permissiveness of North American society. There are no paid sick days during the year. Failure to punch the timeclock invites a verbal reprimand from the foreman or higher supervision. Visiting fellow workers during rotational breaks is discouraged and repeated violations will bring written reprimands (recorded on the employee's record).

Leaves of absence (without pay) are frowned upon and workers denied such leaves are not entitled to an explanation for the denial. Leaves are granted by the personnel manager, superintendent, and general foreman. If any of the supervisors involved harbours a personal dislike for a worker leave is usually refused. One employee was denied a leave of absence to visit aging relatives in Ireland. Frustrated and disillusioned the worker returned two weeks late from a model-change-over plant shutdown. He had gone to Ireland anyway without an official leave of absence. As a punitive measure the employee was fired (losing all his seniority) then rehired as a new employee, and placed in a less desirable job. The worker lost not only his original job but hundreds of dollars in vacation money and benefits. Months later it was learned that leave had been refused because management considered the worker arrogant.

Auto-industry management views hourly-rate employees with great contempt. Nowhere is this more obvious than in the costly, absurd and totally hypocritical "zero defects" and quality control campaigns. Departments and workers are encouraged to compete against each other to determine who can achieve the best quality control. Information pamphlets are distributed, charts gauging improvements or errors are made and "pep talks" are conducted in department offices. One such competition was called "operation steak" (I suspend the narrative for a moment of derision) with the winning department being "treated" to a T-bone steak as a reward for increased productivity and fewer defects. B. F. Skinner would be hard-pressed to come up with something as grisly. Some workers actually supported the contest causing much inter-departmental rivalry and friction. As an added incentive, individuals and groups who had exceeded work norms or discovered errors made by fellow workers were allowed the "privilege" of being photographed with the plant manager or some other notable. A display area was constructed where the pictures were exhibited along with the zero defects car of the week. Even workers' children were encouraged to get into the act by designing posters for the quality control campaign. Winning posters were chosen by management who supplied captions such as "start your day the zero defects way," "quality work comes from healthy people," "a healthy worker is a happy worker," et hoc genus omne ad nauseam.

The hypocrisy of the quality control campaign becomes evident whenever there is a sudden increase of new car orders. Production lines run faster but the workload of assembly operators remains the same or is reduced only slightly. During the "speed-ups" quality declines rapidly. Inspectors discover more damaged or missing parts but any complaints voiced about line speed are virtually ignored. The automobile industry preaches quality control during slack times but any increase in sales and production exposes the programme as little more than a fraudulent public relations gimmick.

The company suggestion plan is another scheme which often exploits naive workers. By catering to people's need for "recognition" and "achievement" the company obtains ideas at bargain basement rates. One blue collar employee at General Motors suggested that all pay-cheques be inscribed with the slogan "G. M. is your company, buy and boost G. M. products". A grievance was filed by several employees who complained that the inscription was misleading since G. M. is neither owned nor controlled by its workers. Management informed the union that the hourly-rate employee who submitted the suggestion had already been paid. To remove the inscription the union would have to take action against one of its own members. The grievance was dropped and the inscription remains on the weekly pay-cheque, a legacy of the highly-touted suggestion plan which rewards "inventiveness" and "benefits everybody involved". Some overzealous employees have made suggestions which, if implemented, would eliminate the jobs of fellow workers.

Job safety is another area where public relations techniques have triumphed. Workers are urged to report any unsafe practices or conditions to the plant "safety man" (an unqualified person usually chosen from the office staff). Many workers assume that the safety man's job is to investigate complaints and suggest corrective measures. The real purpose of the job is to prevent any costly disability or compensation claims which might be filed by injured workers. This is done by making the work area "technically" safe (e.g., warning markers, safety glasses, gloves, ear plugs, steel capped shoes, etc.). It is cheaper than changing dangerous work procedures or faulty equipment. It is also a simple way to enhance the safety conscious image that the automobile industry likes to project.

The most depressing aspect of life in an automobile factory is the relationship between lower level management (department foremen) and hourly-rate employees. A department foreman is usually responsible for the deployment of personnel in a specific area. It is the foreman who familiarizes new employees with plant routine and the job to be assigned. A senior employee or utility man (so named because of his ability to do any job on the line) remains with the new worker to demonstrate how the particular job is done. The alloted time to learn the job, as agreed upon by management and the union, is three days. In very few cases does the utility man remain with the "newhire" for the full three day period. As soon as basic competence is achieved the worker is left alone to do the job. In many cases the ability is acquired within the first few hours on the job. Since work on the assembly line involves a repetition of several simple mechanical tasks many foremen are often disturbed when a newhire requires more than a day to learn the job. Some pressure may be applied to hasten the worker's learning process. The new employee may be taken to a plant office and asked if any personal problems are affecting his performance. From the outset the employee realizes that the foreman's job is not to manage people but to check and nag them. If a new employee fails to learn the job in the allowed period he may be transferred from job to job, upsetting established personnel. The resulting confusion often produces situations where older employees are moved into more strenuous positions. The senior employee files a grievance with the shop committeeman (union representative) who discusses the problem with the foreman. A heated debate often ensues and hours can be spent haggling over seniority rights.

One such incident involved a tall senior employee who had been assigned to a less desirable job in the pit section of the final assembly area (one of the worst jobs in the plant). The pit was approximately five feet nine inches deep and the worker stood six feet tall. It was obvious that the man would be forced to work in an awkward, uncomfortable position. A grievance was filed after the foreman refused to move the man to a more suitable position. The plant doctor was summoned and the worker was compelled to stand up against the wall and be measured (like a horse). It was agreed that the man was too tall and the doctor suggested that a different job would be more appropriate. The foreman refused to consider the suggestion, complaining that other jobs were simply unavailable. The imbroglio which developed involved the union, the plant doctor, and three levels of management. The problem was finally solved when the worker went on a two week sick leave suffering from severe neck pains. Many work hours were lost by treating men as interchangeable spare parts in a gigantic well-oiled machine. The wasted time and residual ill-feeling could have been avoided by allowing the newhire sufficient time to learn the original job or by raising the salary for the less desirable job, increasing the chance of some voluntary change of position. Management decried such alternatives as "inefficient" and "costly" but the time and money lost in grievance procedures and sick leave was considered normal.

When a new employee becomes accustomed to a job an attempt will be made to increase productivity and "work output". The foreman usually approaches the worker with some pressing problem which, it is confided, can only be solved with the participation and co-operation (favourite words in the auto-industry) of the employee involved. Participation usually means that the workload will be increased. A worker soon discovers that his job, which previously was easy, becomes progressively more difficult as several new tasks are added to the routine. The supervisor explains that the increased workload is only temporary but months later the worker is still burdened with the extra tasks. If an attempt is made by the union to lessen the workload, supervision will summon the time study analysts who invariably see management's point of view. The section foreman consoles the worker by disclaiming any responsibility for the increased workload, preferring instead to shift the blame to his immediate supervisors who, he claims, "don't understand the problems on the line". In this manner responsibility never rests on the individuals but instead is diffused throughout the hierarchy. It is an effective way to increase productivity while avoiding outright conflicts between lower level management and hourly-rate employees.

The avoidance of individual responsibility has become an art in the automobile industry. Even the lowliest section foreman has a scapegoat when something goes wrong. The department foreman has an assistant (the utility man) who often relays information from the supervisors to the workers on the line. If a contentious issue develops the foreman will often confide to certain workers that the utility man has relayed false information so as to discredit management. It is an effective way to channel hourly-rate discontent away from management since workers assume, often correctly, that the utility man will do anything to obtain a promotion. The situation produces tension (the utility man is an hourly-rate dues paying union member) which often leads to bitter interdepartmental feuds. Management is made aware of the infighting and often acts as a final mediator or "disinterested third party".

The militaristic attitudes of the automobile industry are in direct conflict with union efforts to humanize the work-place. Tensions will increase with the influx of younger, less docile workers. In an effort to placate dissatisfied workers management has created human relations departments in several plants. The new departments provide a counselling service for workers who wish to "air their beefs". Other functions include the showing of inspirational films (with themes that emphasize the necessity of working each and every day, beating the foreign competitors, pride in workmanship) and dissemination of company literature, usually pamphlets which subtly remind workers that they are part of the labour aristocracy. Management uses every opportunity to propagandize about benefit plans, high salaries, and all the other "goodies" which were obtained through collective bargaining. The industry's initial opposition to all progressive schemes is rarely mentioned. Some plants have introduced Muzak sound systems to "entertain" the workers while they toil. The bland, middle of the road music wafts through the air producing an eerie Kafkaesque scene as the men sweat and strain on the shop floor below. Most workers realize that any attempt made, by management, to improve working conditions is purely cosmetic in nature. The absurdity of most human relations programmes is obvious even to the most dedicated of company apologists. It is only through some form of workers' self-management that working conditions can be genuinely humanized.

To achieve that, political mobilization assumes prime importance since management will resist, with great vigour, any threat to its profit generating production processes. At present, the political impulses of workers are dissipated by the repressive, workman-like, non-thinking atmosphere that prevails in most plants. Many young workers express their discontent through chronic absenteeism and random sabotage but the great majority of men remain unmoved and resigned to their fate. The establishment of a permissive climate would allow workers the luxury of political debate. Some plant managers prohibit workers from reading the daily newspapers during plant hours because of the controversial political items that appear. Management feels that inflammatory articles might "upset" workers to the extent where arguments would occur.

At present the average worker is indifferent or hostile to political ideology. This is especially true of the labour aristocracy where "commodity fetishism" reigns supreme. Every effort is made to divert the intellectual energy of workers into safe, acceptable forms of expression. Car trading, home repair, athletic activity, the obsession with gadgetry, television viewing, excessive socializing, heavy drinking (unless it affects work performance) are "harmless" pastimes which deflect or suppress the restlessness and frustrations of workers. Management willingly supports any activity which will absorb the discontent generated by dull work and regimentation. In-plant horseplay is rarely discouraged since it demonstrates to observers that the workers are basically childish and irreponsible, thus invalidating any discussion of worker self-management. The most elaborate psychological camouflage imaginable is employed to discourage the worker from examining his objective life situation. This is accomplished by a vicious job classification system which capitalizes on working class insecurity and feelings of inferiority. Most men enjoy some amount of challenge in their job situation but the company twists this natural desire into a divisive, humiliating competition for "prestige" and status. Certain jobs are "classified" and the men who perform the functions are given extra money and job titles (dingman, inspector, metal finisher etc.). The salary difference between classified and non-classified jobs is usually a nominal 10 cents to 20 cents an hour. In many cases the skill required for the classified job is less than that of any other ordinary job. Industrial psychologists (ergo management) "know that a person who is extremely deficient in his sense of self-worth is more vulnerable to manipulation, and is easier to keep in place, than a person who has a great sense of self-worth. There is benefit, then, in keeping social approval a scarce commodity, given to some but not to others." In the automobile industry the job classification system serves as the civilian equivalent of military rank and "pecking order". It is an inexpensive method of keeping everybody on their toes and undercutting any chance of working class fellowship and human solidarity. Workers, who since childhood have been reminded that they are only as good as their job or their paycheque, compete against each other for the esteem of men who regard the working class with utter contempt. This type of self-flagellation fosters a seething resentment, envy and hatefulness. The policy of divide and rule is paramount in the automobile industry because without it, current industrial attitudes could not be perpetuated. It is in management's self-interest to promote working class tensions and divisions. If workers ceased feeling inferior they might question the prevailing production methods, absurd regulations and the whole hierarchical structure of authority. Such a development would completely undermine the present "chiefs and warriors" mentality that so poisons our social relationships.

Once in the United States when the entire leadership of the Industrial Workers of the World was arrested, rank and file Wobblies were asked what they would do without their leaders. "What do you mean," they asked, "without our leaders? We are all leaders." This type of infectious self-confidence is what workers must strive to regain.

To facilitate the development of industrial democracy workers must free themselves of the petty grievances which now consume so much time and energy. Changes or "improvements" can be union negotiated but any radical alternative must emanate from rank and file agitation. Certain tactics and strategies should be adopted to stimulate working class consciousness. Any meaningful proposals should include the reduction of the work week as a preliminary goal. This measure must be designed to increase employment in the industry (hopefully attracting a younger, more aware workforce. Radicals might test Rudi Dutschke's concept of "a long march through the institutions"). A flexible work schedule, the optional work week, could be devised allowing people, depending on their needs, the choice of fifteen, twenty, thirty hour work weeks. The current obsession with a "compressed" work week (fewer days, longer hours) only furthers the growth of packaged leisure time, expensive time occupying activities which are socially acceptable and create a lucrative leisure industry as a side effect. The optional work week would radically threaten the present system of manufactured wants and engineered consumerism by undermining the repressive compartmentalization of work time-free time.

Other measures should include the abolition of penalties for refusing overtime work. Scheduled and unscheduled overtime should be on a voluntary basis only. Leaves of absence (without pay) should be granted upon request, avoiding arbitrary judgments based on alleged personality defects or non-conforming attitudes. Bells, buzzers, sirens and other Pavlovian devices should be eliminated from plant life.

A workers' council must have the right to oversee all hiring, firing, demotion, transfers and work assignments. This council must also participate and have veto power in any decisions involving lay-offs, plant closures or relocation, product pricing, pension funds, insurance, supplementary unemployment benefits, production line speeds, job safety, shift determination, time-motion studies, plant expansion, job classifications, skilled trades apprenticeships, vacations, bereavement pay, grievances, job evaluation, discipline, overtime, salaries, cafeteria management, advertising, plant security, work schedules, etc.

The creation of a worker sponsored education and information committee is essential. Any worker seeking advice on credit buying, social problems, and individual rights would have available, at all times, a free consultation service. It would also provide a forum for discussion of political and economic problems affecting the larger community. Workers must also counter any false, public relations inspired company propaganda by exposing facts about profits, dividends, and relations with government.

An independent automobile industry must be developed with all manufacturing processes located in Canada. Decisions made in Detroit or Washington often affect, adversely, thousands of Canadian autoworkers.

Canadian workers must also create unions which are not dominated by American money or influence. Master agreements or contracts negotiated by the international union (located in Detroit) often reflect the priorities of the American economy. Fringe benefits such as denticare, health insurance, prescription eyeglasses, and supplementary unemployment benefits are more important to American workers since the U.S. economy is less "socialized" than Canada's. Such schemes are becoming increasingly irrelevant to Canadian workers as government expands its social security role. Canadian workers not only lose the value of any benefits negotiated by the international union but also pay higher taxes as the result of increased state paternalism. This trend became evident in the recently completed UAW "Big Three" negotiations. Major issues were pensions, dental care and voluntary overtime. By downplaying wage demands and concentrating on fringe benefits, UAW President Leonard Woodcock was determined to play the role of "labour statesman" conforming, in large part, to Dick Nixon's anti-labour Phase Four guidelines on wages. This means that Canadian workers will bear the brunt of ever increasing prices with an inferior contract negotiated for the benefit of American workers — and presidents.

The whole question of a rational, overall transportation system (not necessarily of the internal combustion variety) must not be ignored. The worth of the automobile industry must, eventually, be examined critically, with the emphasis on devising effective alternative modes of transportation, concentrating existing technology on such a goal.

Workers must assume more control over their own lines. Manipulation by the media, plant management, government, and even the union must be challenged by spontaneous demonstrations or group action. Organizations tend to produce hierarchies and authoritarian reflexes which, if left unchecked, create élitist, anti-worker sentiment.

In an affluent, highly technological society there is no good reason why workers should remain chained to nineteenth-century industrial attitudes. The enormous profits that the automobile industry declares annually make management reluctant to tamper with existing methods and conditions. It must be workers who act as the catalyst in radically changing the human environment.

Working as a Trade Unionist

interview with Jean Levesque

Johnson:
What is your connection with the International Woodworkers of America?

Levesque:
Well, I'm regional rep for the Woodworkers. That means I'm partly in charge of the Montréal office and responsible for the servicing and organizing of union people in the French-speaking areas of the province. I'm covering an area of two hundred and fifty miles, including places like Montréal, St. Jean, Thurso, and Hawkesbury. For six months of the year, I'm travelling around the province and dealing with workers in small plants, usually furniture plants. Most of these plants employ a hundred people or less, so the problems encountered are quite different from problems you might find in large industrial plants with hundreds of employees. Workers in these small plants just don't have as much power as unionized people who are concentrated in large industrial plants. Most of these small plants are very paternalistic. The workers know the boss directly and, very often, he's not considered an enemy. Workers who have been around fifteen or twenty years, often since a plant started, remember when the boss worked alongside them on the shop floor. As a result, many of the conflicts that arise in these small factories are quite different from the conflicts that arise in a big, traditional capitalist factory, where you have, on one side, people who are getting shafted regularly, and, on the other side, the owners, who are completely unknown by the workers. In the situations I'm involved with, the biggest problem is to make people aware of the differences between workers and owners. The basic problem that faces workers in small shops is the arbitrary authority of the bosses. As it is now, most workers are not intellectuals and the fact is that most union contracts are written by intellectuals. The clauses in the contracts are quite complicated and many workers just don't know their rights. Workers are faced with that lack of knowledge and their own lack of knowledge, and the fact that the foreman or the plant manager is using the respect the

Jean Levesque is a regional representative for the International Woodworkers of America, and lives in Montréal.

workers have for them to explain to the workers how they see their rights. The foreman or the manager is going to interpret the contract in a way which is the most favourable to the management position. For example, most of the present contracts limit the amount of overtime that can be worked and, usually, anything over the schedule fortyhour week must be voluntary. Well, it very often happens that the company representative or foreman will ask a worker if he wants to work overtime. If the guy is not interested that day, the boss might never ask him again. It's finished as far as the boss is concerned, and he considers the worker a real son of a bitch for refusing. I'm faced with this kind of problem all the time. And it's hard to control, because the company is supposed to give workers equal opportunities for overtime, but if they don't, who will complain? It's hard to get people in a small shop to talk about their grievances. Sometimes, people are afraid, sometimes they aren't aware of their rights and the fact is, that I'm only coming to see the worker once a month, maximum. For the rest of the time, the only contact they have is with the plant committee, which is just not very effective.

Johnson:
Does the plant committee tend to rubberstamp company policies?

Levesque:
No, not exactly, but that is one of the most serious problems we have, not only here, but all over North America. Many workers consider the responsibility involved in belonging to a plant committee as one way to get out of the shop, on one side or the other. Either they become union reps later or foremen.

Johnson:
Because of the knowledge they have acquired by working as a union rep, they are more capable of assuming management positions.

Levesque:
Yeah, of course. Let's face it, the people who are part of the committee are working very hard, exhausting themselves. And to do that you have to be strong, you have to be active, and you have to be bright too. And, of course, the company is interested in having those kinds of people on its side. For example, I recently received a phone call from a woman who is President of a local that I deal with. Well, she's a fantastic woman. She's been fighting the company for months and exhausting the management representatives. She has proved herself so adept at handling management, that they have offered her the position of personnel manager with the company. She called me and asked my advice about this. Well, what can I say to that woman? As it is now, she's just working as a packer. It's an awful job. Here's a chance for her to have a top job in the plant. How can I advise her? Well, I just can't give her

any advice. On the one hand, she's going to take her knowledge of the union and the union procedures to management, but, on the other hand, if she doesn't take the job, she is going to be stuck with routine work for the rest of her life.

Johnson:
Is most of the work in this industry of a routine nature?

Levesque:
Well, there are two kinds of plants. The work in furniture plants requires more craftsmanship than work in the production area. On the other hand, there are production workers, like the woman I just mentioned, producing things like foam cups, who are really alienated if you look at them from the outside. But it's quite difficult to make these people aware of their own alienation. For example, let's talk about that woman who has been very militant and active over the past couple of years. She has been a real thorn in the company's side, yet, on the other hand, she called me a month ago, and was very proud to tell me that she had just worked thirty-two consecutive hours. Jesus Christ! Thirty-two hours straight. That means a whole day and night, and then another eight hours. She had a better job than the one she normally has, which is awful. It was quality control, which is easier but, hell, thirty-two hours sitting in a small box, controlling those stupid little cups, it's crazy. But she was proud. She didn't feel that she was being used badly. And most of the workers I'm dealing with feel that way. And there are reasons for this attitude. What do they have, apart from their job? They are living in some stinking suburb. The woman, for example, is not very happy with her marriage. The work is a refuge for her because it's a place to go other than her home. She's happy to go to work. She doesn't have anything to do at home. Most workers don't have many outside interests. If you think about it, what does a suburb like Chomedy, as an example, give the people culturally or intellectually? And the workers are not conditioned to have outside interests. These are people who never read any books.

Johnson:
Part of the reason for that, I suppose, is because they're too tired after work?

Levesque:
That's right, it's a vicious circle. You're too tired to read a book but, on the other hand, you'll never become dissatisfied with the situation that makes you too tired, because you won't read books. If you were reading books, you'd be more likely to become dissatisfied with what you're doing.

Johnson:
Do you think that when people like us are dealing with other workers who don't have a feeling of dissatisfaction over a routine job, we tend to project our own feelings onto them when we're dealing with them?

Levesque:
Well, we're all human beings, and I don't think it's human to sit down at a table for thirty-two hours straight and control the quality of paper cups. It's crazy! And it's not just a projection of my prejudices, imagining myself sitting there in her place. To say it's completely inhuman is a normal reaction, I think.

Johnson:
Yet obviously she gets a degree of satisfaction out of it.

Levesque:
Yeah, well the whole society has held the ability to work hard as its highest virtue up until the last generation. And that's not the only problem. For example, when we started to negotiate a contract recently at one plant, we tried to define what the policy would be and what kind of demands to make to improve the situation in the plant. I'm against excessive salary differentiation in the plant. The people are all working in the same plant. Obviously, the guy who has five or six kids has more needs than the guy who is a bachelor, but the father who has five or six kids might be scrubbing the floor and the bachelor, who might have a nicer job, is making three times as much in salary. I'm always fighting, even with the committee, as well as the plant membership, to convince people that everybody has the right to make enough to satisfy their basic needs. Well, it's impossible. A worker who has been employed for one year is completely opposed to the idea that a man who is doing the same work, but only for the last three months, should be receiving the same pay. For the worker who has been around longer, it's not just a question of seniority, it's a question of doing better work.

Johnson:
A question of pride, perhaps. Because he's been there longer and acquired more competency, he feels entitled to more, and if you mention to him, that this other guy is entitled to the same wage by virtue of his needs, he doesn't understand.

Levesque:
Exactly. It's out of the question. It's hard to get the one year employee to recognize that it really only takes three months to learn the job, and if a guy does the same work, he should get the same pay.

Johnson:
Part of the reason, I suppose, is because people attach so much of their self-image and self-worth to the job they are doing. They feel insulted if

someone comes up and says a guy can learn the same job you've been on for a year in two or three months.

Levesque:
Definitely. So, I try to push libertarian socialist ideas in the labour movement. Let's face it, the labour movement is really one of the few... Hell, it's the only force that the working class has in society even if it's badly used. What good am I if I just concern myself with economic issues, and avoid the problems and conflicts that result from the kind of society we live in? Look at that woman I was telling you about before. As I said before, what does she have in her suburb? Just the shit that's on television. The infantile crap that we get from Channels 10 and 2 (Montréal French language television stations). So what interests does she have except for her work? Is it any wonder that she boasts to me that she has worked thirty-two hours straight? I really believe you have to get involved with people, not only at the workplace, but in their outside lives as well. For example, the people I am working with, I consider friends until they show me that they're not. Well, I invited that woman a couple of times to my house. For her it was a fantastic experience, because she was exposed to an entirely different lifestyle. It was crazy to her. I don't know if that changed anything for her but, at least, it made her question her lifestyle. Other things happened that made me think that her attitude had changed. For example, the guy who was Vice-President of the union local during the strike, who was very militant and became good friends with her and me, had an accident. He lost four fingers on his left hand, so he's on unemployment, and not getting much from Compensation. Well, the woman is working six days a week and giving him one day's pay. She may have done it if I had never been in contact with her, but I think that, through things we have discussed, she finds it's not only because he's a friend, it's also because he's a worker. Because there are reasons now, beside friendship, that justify her helping that guy. She would probably help any other worker in the plant who really needed it.

Johnson:
So she has come to accept the libertarian concept of mutual aid?

Levesque:
Yeah, she did. Even if I resigned from my union work now, I'd think that was something positive.

Johnson:
Is there much of this mutual aid among workers you've met, or is there competitiveness?

Levesque:
Well, there is definitely a competitiveness, which is created and used by the society and by the employers. The best examples of that are

plants which operate on an incentive plan. That's the worst kind of competition. Not only are workers urged to compete against each other, but also against themselves. A guy wakes up in the morning and says to himself, "I have to make money because I have to live, so if I want to have extra money, I have to work harder than yesterday and tomorrow harder than today." For example, in a production plant, people depend on each other very much. I'm at one point on the production line, and I'm waiting on the product that's coming from another point. If the bastard before me doesn't work, I won't make any money. That's the problem. The only time when people have any real degree of solidarity is when they go on strike. There is no more work, so the factor that makes the competition so bad is removed. And then, of course, you can start to change people's minds. During a strike, I'm always trying to have as many people as possible involved in what's happening. Let's face it, a contract will engage people in a process which will last two or three years so it's very important to have frequent meetings with the membership. After all, it's their contract, it's their wages and working conditions, it's their lives. They have to fight to get it and they'll be bound with it when the union reps aren't around. I'm against the idolizing or fetishizing of the plant committee and the union rep. I'm aware of my limits and try to criticize my role as often as possible but a worker who, by election, becomes a member of the negotiating committee brings a lot of unhealthy baggage with him. For him it's quite a different experience, sitting around a table, sometimes twelve hours at a stretch without having a meal. It's very hard for a worker who is used to having his meals regularly, to work eight hours and to be paid overtime if he works over that. It's a lot different from what he's used to, and he often does a lot of bullshitting which is of no value. That's what I mean by unhealthy baggage. Sometimes he is exploiting his position by pretending he is the victim of the whole group. He might say, "I'm doing that for you." That's what he's telling his co-workers.

Johnson:
Do you think a worker who gets a position in the union hierarchy or bureaucracy uses this position positively or negatively?

Levesque:
Well, sometimes he's using it as a step to become foreman, or union rep, but during the period that he is doing the work, it's usually positive. You know, there are two sides to a coin. Being on the plant committee is a temporary thing. Only a person who has decided from the start that he's a militant, and that he will never be anything other than a militant will remain that way. And that is very rare. Usually, a guy uses his position to further himself in some way, but, on the other hand, what he's doing may still have positive results.

94

Johnson:

Is there a tendency to be less militant or perhaps come to see things management's way, because of being raised above the rest of the workers?

Levesque:

No, I don't think so. He's raised above the ordinary worker, but on the worker's side. It's not a change in mentality, but there is a recognition of the importance of hierarchy and power in our society. But that's true of most people in society, this power tripping impulse. But that's not a change in mentality, it's just the worker trying to justify the fact that he has that sense of power.

Johnson:

What have you done to encourage rank and file workers to develop their own criticisms of the company and to take certain actions?

Levesque:

Well, that's a very good question because, in fact, it's a very difficult problem for a union rep.

Johnson:

Because you're placed in a position above rank and file workers. You're almost like a priest.

Levesque:

Exactly. It's very difficult to convince people that you're just a human being like them. I haven't been to university, I was just a worker who became a union rep, but to convince people of that is something else. As a concrete example, I'm presently trying to de-mystify the position of plant committee member or, more importantly, the union rep. We are negotiating a new contract now for six hundred people. What we're planning to do is to ask the committee to negotiate publicly. There's nothing to hide under the table. Everything is open on our side. We'll rent the local arena and negotiate on the stage so that everybody will see what's going on. Now, of course, there'll have to be some discipline, hopefully self-discipline, because it's impossible to negotiate if six hundred people are yelling and screaming at once. If people will agree to discipline themselves, I'll fight like hell to arrange this meeting so as to get people involved as voyeurs. Involved enough so that when we meet with the membership and talk about the negotiations, they'll have a better understanding of what we are talking about. At least they'll know that there is nothing sacred or mystical about what is going on in that room when we are negotiating. The problem is that many union reps prefer to have private meetings with the company.

Johnson:

Because they can get away with more than they could if meetings were public.

Levesque:
No, I was referring to something even worse than that. I'm talking about people who are selling their souls. It happens from time to time. It was shown in the construction industry in Québec that there are crooks and gangsters in the union. But why especially in the union and not elsewhere? There are crooks in business, so why not in the unions?

Johnson:
You're trying to develop a rank and file consciousness that will eventually make the position of union rep unnecessary, to encourage people to make known their demands and really influence things. What is the resistance to this? Is it a psychological problem stemming from the feelings of inferiority that have been bred into the working class because of the society, the environment, the family and the hierarchical order of things? Workers have been conditioned to feel inferior and have trouble asserting themselves and making demands on the company. Is that true?

Levesque:
That's true.

Johnson:
Well, what can you do to break that down? How do you give people the feeling that they can change things themselves?

Levesque:
First of all, I try to point out to workers that I am just a resource person. I can't negotiate for them on my own. I'm only valuable because I know some of the tricks management uses against the workers so I'm at their service as far as information goes, but I'm always pointing out the fact that it's their contract and their life. And, for example, if there's a grievance, I'll ask the guys what the situation is around that machine. And then they realize that they know something that I don't know. I'm asking them questions. They explain the situation to me and they are proud of what they know. They know more in that area than I know. And that's only normal because I'm not in the plant. But, on the other hand, I feel my contribution is important too. Last week, I was working with a group that's trying to negotiate a new contract with the company. They were trying to revise the whole salary scale. Well, that's good but it's important to remember that the company is going to want to hear some justification for the changes. Again, the best paid people got the best adjustments and the low paid people the worst. Well, this is something you've got to fight against because they're calculating the increases in percentages usually. So I ask the guys what their justifications for the increases were. They said the increases were justified by the jump in the cost of living. Well, the cost of living is hurting the guy who's making $2.10 an hour a hell of a lot more than the guy who's making $4.50.

By increasing everybody's wage by the same percentage, you're not really helping the guy who's hurt most by inflation. We should be trying to close the gap between wages in the shop. Well, the guys are beginning to realize that we have to work together. I have nothing more to give them than they have to give me. It's a symbiotic relationship.

Johnson:
There's a great deal of talk now by the federal government about this concept of industrial democracy. This means that workers would have more control over the work they do as well as the work environment. At its extreme this would mean that workers would have a direct influence on the way an enterprise was managed. Do you think that's possible, given the present consciousness of working people? If so, would it be desirable?

Levesque:
No. Workers are not prepared to do that now. Most workers are conditioned to sit down on their ass, or to work as slaves and to let other people do the thinking and present them with a blueprint for change. If that happened now, I think it would just be a trap that management would use. Just like they are now using the contract to explain to workers their rights, as they see it, because the worker doesn't read the contract. You only give the workers the illusion of democracy, but the basic psychology of each worker has not been changed. Working class people are made to feel inferior, to feel like second class citizens. If they didn't feel that way, they wouldn't put up with the garbage that's heaved at them now. And that's one of the biggest problems I've encountered, how to break down that feeling of inferiority. In my efforts, I'm always trying to help workers have a better self-image and a better understanding of their worth to society. And on a larger scale, away from the job as well. A man is not only a worker, he also lives sixteen hours a day away from the job. I think it's very important that people have some connection between what they do at work and what they do away from work. In other words, outside influences have an effect on a person, not only as a worker, but also as a human being, citizen, and member of society. Once these things start happening, the work environment will be fundamentally changed. Once people have some demands and these demands aren't satisfied, it's just like a snowball, it can't be stopped. The worker who starts to go to Cinema Outremont (a Montréal theatre), because there are many good films there, becomes a different kind of worker. He will no longer be content with the mindless pap on Channel Ten or Channel Two. That's the difference between a worker who thinks, and a slave. The development of democracy at the community level (tenants unions, consumer unions, neighbourhood councils) will spread to the workplace. Class consciousness and struggle will affect the neighbourhoods in turn. We cannot separate the worker into two parts. It's the same fight.

Working in a Social Agency

by Lucia Kowaluk

Social workers consider themselves professionals. In addition to the dictionary definition, this implies a freedom to move, to use judgement, to act according to one's best judgement. It also implies a self-directedness and a say in and responsibility for one's working conditions, and the policy under which one works. People with energy and intelligence go into social work, not as much for the money, as for the chance to be self-directing in their work.

Human beings like to feel they are in control of their work, that they understand the meaning it reflects, and that they can see the results. These feelings, as much as anything else, draw people into the professions. *201756*

But when we look at how social work is being practised, we have to question the way it is being offered, the way it is being run, and the degree to which the worker is involved in directing his/her own work.

Social work — that is, the discipline represented by several years of formal training at an accredited institution — teaches the recipient a combination of skills which are: the insight to define human dynamics, internally and as they relate in small social groups like the family, and intervention in these dynamics (if the dynamics are creating problems) in such a way as to change those relationships. Additional skills involve a knowledge of the community and how people relate to that community, and intervention into that relationship so that it can be helpful.

Lucia Kowaluk has been a social worker for fifteen years and has worked as a family case worker and community organiser as well as a supervisor for social agencies in Montréal.

Social work defined in this way is — on the whole — practised through agencies in the community. Over the past 50 years these agencies have changed their focus several times, from concern with social conditions to concern with individuals or their affinity groups, to the point now where a combination of the two exists, sometimes within one agency and usually with the result that tension is created within the agency.

Social work, on the whole, is a profession with specialties in solving problems, usually by resolving conflict. Although there is a respectable wing of social work that attempts to resolve individual and family problems with very aggressive techniques of highlighting conflicts, most social workers by temperament and training do not use these techniques. There is also an even smaller faction of social work which attempts to use aggressive techniques to solve community problems such as organizing welfare recipients to sit-in at welfare offices, but this faction is an even smaller minority.

By and large, social workers by temperament and training are not geared to seeing situations in terms of *irreconcilable* conflicts (put in more political terms, they have no class analysis), and this fact, more than any other, leaves them ill-equipped to fight the battle for workers' control which they are slowly losing.

There are other elements as well. Social workers, on the whole, come from middle class backgrounds (largely because of their educational requirements), and nothing in their training has taught them to analyze the role of the middle class in our society. Notions that the needs and goals of workers, in any industry or organization, are opposed to the needs and goals of management are very unfamiliar to them. Social workers have been very slow to unionize for the simple reason that they have never seen themselves as opposed to the management of their agencies.

This failure to understand a class struggle in our society has often made social workers, while compassionate and liberal in their individual relationships with clients, conservative in their broader social and political position. That is, they have not understood the underlying struggle that goes on between working class or lumpen-proletariat ("multi-problem families", in social work jargon) consumers of service, and the social agencies and social workers in them. Social workers as individuals are genuinely hurt and shocked when it is suggested that they and their agencies represent class interests opposed to the interests of the working class clients the agencies serve.

The simplest example concerns money. Social workers are paid, among other things, to administer money for poor people. In the old days they (Red Feather) literally dispersed funds which came from the donations of employers who didn't pay a decent wage to their working class employees in the first place. Now social workers police the management of tax-raised welfare funds. They either parcel out the whole welfare cheque of a family or they give "extras" that come from volunteer donations. This is an untenable situation for all involved. Social work literature is full of rationalization in defense of this police work, and poor people react in ways ranging from repressed rage and frustration which manifests itself in depression, to outright anger and lying. This is labeled "manipulation" and it's no holds barred in the struggle which ensues between social worker and client.

Of course this struggle over money is not involved with middle class or working class families who have steady and decent incomes, which is the main reason why agencies are turning more and more to "counselling" — a valid and useful line of work but one which is conceptually much easier to deal with than the struggle against poverty, in which, without an understanding of the roles of classes in our society, the social worker is caught in a trap, with his/her loyalties torn between the client and the agency. A social worker is taught to be loyal first to the agency (the institution) rather than to the client, exactly the opposite as in the legal or medical professions (e.g., no lying about money, share all information with supervisors).

Usually when a social worker tries to shift the loyalty by urging clients to give their opinions and share control, the flood-gates of rage open, and the social worker her/himself becomes the first recipient of the attack, both because he/she is the most visible and handy, and because he/she had been an accomplice in shutting working class people out of control. From personal experience I can say that this is a very shocking and hurtful experience, often not tried again. And then the tentative alliance between social worker and client-consumer-recipient-of-service to struggle against poverty and propertied control in this society sinks into a quagmire of hurt and confused feelings.

But the spectre is rising again. Social work agencies, traditionally small and closely and personally linked to their own management, and their sources of funding (United Appeal, etc.) are becoming larger and linked to bigger and bigger bureaucracies. The sources of funding are more and more the provincial governments. The details of the growth of these bureaucracies vary from province to province, so for one example we will deal with Québec.

The non-governmental bureaucracies both control a large number of agencies, and at the same time are answerable to the government in their basic policies and their expenditure of money. As thousands, indeed millions, of dollars become available for new offices and staff to manage and boss this bureaucracy, people at the community level (mothers asking for day-care, teen-agers needing drop-in centres, and social workers themselves looking frantically on a Friday afternoon for a place to put an abandoned child for the weekend) are told that the province has no funds to set up these resources.

If there ever was a time for social workers to fight for control over their jobs, it is now. Bureaucracy and control from above brings with it more problems than it solves. Bureaucracy and over-all control is defended by stating the need to co-ordinate services and pool resources, thus saving money. Over-all control may, indeed, co-ordinate services, but if the co-ordination is governed by policies which recipients of services (now called "consumers"), and the givers of services (the social workers) do not create; and if, once the policies are made, they cannot be changed because the people who see the need for change have no access to the top, then the co-ordination is simply oppressive. As for saving money, the bureaucracy costs more money than it is saving.

Bureaucracy creates a malaise among workers. Far from helping mothers work efficiently and quickly, it has the effect of either cutting them off from direct contact with the community (symbolized by the sterile, glass, high-rise buildings which house their offices, completely out of touch with reality) that needs service, or it offers a morass of lines of decision-making to the worker who wants to respond quickly to needs he/she has perceived through direct contact with the community.

"The real reasons for the present structure are discernable, though hidden. The organizations are power-ridden, and thus the purpose of the system is not efficiency as such, but efficiency of control. We live in a society in which power is to a high degree co-ordinated, not in a terroristic-political fashion, but rather in a manipulative, economic-technical fashion... Exploitation goes on behind a façade of bureaucratic administration wherein power is concealed, distant and highly rationalized". (Benello — "Wasteland Culture", *Our Generation,* Vol. 5, # 1, p. 23).

What is the most shocking and unacceptable about these social work bureaucracies is that they are governed by the values of big business — "management theory" — whose goals are to exploit labour and make profits. It is a compounded tragedy that social agencies, whose expressed goal is to serve people, should adopt these same values of the need for a hierarchy and top-down methods of giving orders.

The supervisory system — an integral part of traditional social work practice within an agency or hospital setting — is the best example of the parallels between social work and business. Beginning with the very valid need for consultation when practice and recommendations are made which affect people's lives and rights, this need has been fit into a system in which social workers are closely watched and ordered to take or not take certain courses of action. Although within a given agency, this boss system may not be used overtly, and while it is true that some individuals, either supervisors or workers, struggle together to work as an equalitarian team, the fact is always clear and in the back of everyone's mind that the basic policies are made at the top, that the supervisor's job is to police those policies, and that the worker in the field is expected to conform.

It is clear indeed that the goal of bureaucracy is efficiency of control, and this is as true of a social agency as it is of big business.

One can speculate as to the reasons why a social agency — which does not have profits at stake — would want to set up — and defend — a system of hierarchical control. Some of the reasons are cultural. We live in a hierarchical society with values that stress individual competitiveness rather than group co-operation. For several individuals to want to get and hold control and maintain a structure to help them do so is culturally inbred. Few of us have skills in helping each other as a total group to make a collective decision which will be carried out by the group and to which we will feel bound. Few of us feel mandated by a group of peers, and instead will wait for orders from a boss.

There can be other reasons, too, like the desire to keep social work practice as a stronghold of professionals. Social work is now being opened to para-professionals. This is a situation which, more than anything else, threatens the *class base* of those who practice. Because of educational requirements (four years of university before two years of social work school), professional social workers tend overwhelmingly to come from the middle or upper middle class. As mentioned above, they carry their class biases and loyalties. Para-professionals, because they have fewer educational requirements (high school leaving and two years at a CEGEP or junior college), tend to come from the working class. They also carry their class biases and loyalties. People from two different classes look differently at the questions of distribution of society's wealth and power — for example, the extent to which those who have it or who don't have it "deserve" their status. These differences in attitude can, obviously, create conflict in the profession of social work, raising many issues. An attempt to control this conflict, for example, is exercised when management insists on "discussing problems" separately with the M.S.W. professionals, from the para-professionals like homemakers and the clerical workers.

Within the bureaucratic hierarchy, supervisory positions are reserved exclusively for M.S.W. (Master of Social Work) professionals (and well socialized ones, at that). The control exercised by the bureaucracy and these loyal workers, the supervisors, ensures that the para-professionals, with their different perspective, will never be in a position to influence policy in any way.

In Montreal, another reason for structured controlling bureaucracies is to keep the language divisions intact. The English agencies stay segregated and under one roof. This answers both the English establishment's desire to maintain a strong institutionalized English presence in Montreal, a fortress, as it were, and the French establishment's desire to keep English-speaking people both the professionals and the consumers ghettoized with their own services. In a multi-lingual city like Montreal there are immigrant families who get caught between the two major language groups — e.g. Italian parents learn French on the job, and their children go to English schools. Unilingual agencies shift these families back and forth, each refusing to serve them for practical or policy reasons. The English agencies say they cannot talk to the parents of these families, and the French agencies, which tend to have bilingual staff, will not serve a family which is part of the English system, meaning their children are in English schools. It is clear that for practical reasons individual social workers and the citizens they serve could work most quickly and comfortably in small, bilingual (or multilingual community-based service centres. If this is so, why do the services remain highly centralized, unilingual and out of reach?

But, finally, when we ask ourselves why social agencies, whose job it is to serve, should adopt the values and management systems of big corporations, whose goals are exploitation and profit, we need only think back on the policing role regarding money that was given to social workers. This "compounded tragedy" should not come as a surprise at all. Social workers are now being asked to be loyal to a bureaucracy whose goal is efficiency of control, both of themselves and of those they "serve". Social workers *must* ask themselves in whose interests they are being asked to serve this bureaucracy.

A simple call for "workers' control" to social workers in agencies and hospitals is shallow in its analysis and weak in its strategy.

If there ever was a time when consumers of services and social workers in the field could form an alliance it is now. The control over workers in the field is less personal than it ever was, and is therefore easier to analyze clearly. It is clearer now than ever that the control is both far removed from the recipient and is in the interests of preserving the status quo vis-à-vis distribution of power and resources in this society.

It is also easier now than ever for social workers to feel for themselves the impotent rage and hurt at being controlled from afar that has plagued many other groups in our society which often show up as consumers of service.

Social workers, like everyone else, are struggling endlessly and conscientiously with the dilemma of working for reform within the system, or chucking it all in favour of establishing counter-institutions. The key answer is what will be the result in actual re-distribution of re-sources and power.

Social workers and consumers must first understand that there is a great deal of wealth in Quebec, enough for good hospital care, plenty of attention to troubled children, recreation and so on. We no longer live with scarcity; we live with mal-distribution. The question to which a social work/consumer alliance must address itself is how to effectively join the fray which decides the priorities for the distribution of those resources. That alliance has not been invited to join into the decision-making process, nor will it ever be. It will never be asked to join because the priorities of consumers are for a bigger share of the pie than the present decision-makers are prepared to give. The fact that a hand-ful of social workers are now by invitation on the fringes of that de-cision-making must be seen for what it is: a few individuals who can be trusted not to rock the boat but to defend the present distribution of power as being a just one, especially since a lot of it is funnelled through them.

As a beginning, social workers with integrity should refuse to be part of those few. "The split between the administrator and the pro-fessional is exacerbated (in bureaucracies) and built-in, and the waste-land culture is institutionalized in big organizations through inequitable distribution of the scarce values of prestige and power, which cluster disproportionately at the top. While the professional derives satisfac-tion predominantly from his work, the administrator derives satisfaction from the control of people within the organizational apparatus" (Be-nello — "Wasteland Culture", *Our Generation*, Vol. 5, #1, p. 24). In practical terms, social workers should refuse to work in any way except in giving direct service. If they choose to be supervisors with a gen-uine teaching consultative role, they must make their loyalties clear from the beginning, both to themselves and to those with whom they have contact. There is a difference between being a consultant who helps social workers in the field work out the best method of procedure to serve the community and being a supervisor who is part of the polic-ing system responsible for seeing that the policy on top is carried out by the "shock troops". Many supervisors are confused about there two roles and tend to meld them together. Since these two roles are most of the time in conflict, supervisors tend, by default, to slip into the latter role. It is far better that they make a clear decision before that happens.

Within agencies — if it is possible — workers can join with con-sumers to assure that the services the agencies give are those that the community wants and needs. This may result in open conflict between the existing policy of the agency and those who want to change it. The kinds of issues that may give this kind of conflict are the degree to which Intake departments are prepared to respond immediately to re-quests from the community, or policies governing foster placements and foster homes. There are others: the amount of budget spent on fancy offices as opposed to direct services, the extent to which clients/consumers have freedom in choosing a social worker as one chooses a doctor or a lawyer.

Another arena is more public and less personal: that is for community groups to work with social workers to re-establish the services they want and need independently of the agencies, and to demand the money to run them. The government will answer that they are already funding the social service agencies to give these services, and the community will have to show publicly that these services are not being adequately delivered. Examples of this are services to particular ethnic and racial communities which are often (as is the case in Montreal) being organized by the community itself completely independent of the network of established social services, and which deliver a variety of services with a clear advocacy bias. Women's services, youth services, and gay services are other examples. The groups that have already organized to offer these services are completely new and controlled by the groups to whom the services are offered. Social workers with these same biases can work with these small groups, both to deliver services and to make public issue of the fact that money is needed to continue delivering the services. It must be made *clear* and *public* that the government (and thus the tax-payer) is funding large agencies to deliver services and that, by and large, these services are not meeting community needs.

Consumers and social workers can also ally to demand extension of existing services or new services. Examples of these are extended nursing care or housing for the elderly, home nursing care, and emergency placement for children and youth. This struggle must not accept the myth that there is no money for these services, but must enter the debate on priorities for the money that exists. This debate includes the questions of how these priorities are decided, and who decides them and for what ends.

There is nothing new in these struggles. There are social workers who have devoted their lives to them and who are undoubtedly weary by now, having achieved some measure of success. The new element in the continuation of this struggle is the additional struggle for control by workers in the field of their jobs, work conditions and policies governing the execution of their jobs. Whereas in the past urban social workers exercised some measure of control in a personal way because the agencies were small, personal and staffed by one's peers, and often, alas, exercised that control in conflict with their clients, clashing usually because of different class interests rationalized by a plethora of social work literature; whereas in the past workers and management had, or thought they had, common goals, it should be clear by now that this is no longer the case. Social workers in the field have much more in common with their clients than with their bosses. The struggle for social workers to work in an equalitarian way on the job and to participate in making the policies that govern their job, is the same struggle as that of the consumers of services who have always struggled to be treated as equals in receiving the services, and to participate in making the policies that govern the delivery of the services. The struggle is the same because both the social workers and the consumers want an essential re-distribution of power and resources in this society, something which the government-built and government-funded bureaucracy does not want.

Working in an Aircraft Plant

interview with Jean-Marie Gonthier

Johnson:
What are you doing at United Aircraft now?

Gonthier:
I'm still the financial secretary of the local union, and right now I'm also functioning as plant chairman. We're working on the return to work of the strikers and the problem of re-organizing the local union.

Johnson:
So most of your time is spent now with the union. You're not working in the shop itself.

Gonthier:
Oh, no, I get all the time that is necessary to re-organize the local, but I'm still an employee of United Aircraft and I still have to report to the plant.

Johnson:
The strike created headlines and left many problems unresolved. Can you go back and outline the issues which brought about the strike in the first place.

Gonthier:
Well, it's an accumulation of things over the past ten years. The union was certified in late 1963 and we signed the first contract in 1964. The policy of the company is really backward. They are still living in the master-servant era and we are bound here by the policy established south of the border in Hartford, Connecticut. The language in the collective agreement is the same throughout the corporation and the local management lawyer is really only a mouth-piece for American management and has no mandate here. Every decision is taken by a Vice-President who comes up from Hartford during the negotiations. So 1967 was a repetition of 1964. There was a strike. We made an

---

Jean-Marie Gonthier works for Pratt and Whitney (formerly United Aircraft) in Longueil, Québec and has recently been appointed to a commission investigating the garment industry in Montréal.

attempt, it turned out to be a very feeble attempt, to get the company to change its policy. The strike was quite bitter but because of a lack of organization it failed after six weeks. We had over seven hundred scabs after six weeks of the strike and the whole effort collapsed. Maybe, looking back now, it was a mistake to fold after only seven weeks because the majority still supported the strike. But the way it was organized, it was only a matter of time before the whole thing fell through. The bargaining committee at the time decided to recommend acceptance of a wishy washy offer so we went back into the plant to try and rebuild the union. The 1970 negotiations were just for the hell of it. There was no real desire to do anything. People were still feeling the effects of 1967 and there was no way we could muster any militancy. So we signed a collective agreement after exhausting all the legal means of negotiations. Things started to happen in the three years since that agreement was signed, especially in 1973 when we were successful in recruiting new members and convincing people that the union would have to make the fight during the next round of bargaining. So when the negotiations started we were in a very good position.

Johnson:
What were the issues involved that created the militancy?

Gonthier:
The main issue was the attitude of the company. Management's rights and their attitude vis-à-vis those rights. You couldn't question their rights or their decisions. It was even considered a sin to ask any questions. When you were told to jump you had to jump and, as I said before, they were still living in the master-servant era and they felt they had the right to do anything as long as they were paying you the wages that they promised to pay you.

Johnson:
What were the shop floor problems?

Gonthier:
Mainly the attitude of supervision. In many instances we saw things happen that we had not seen since our school days. They still have a merit rating system which is for the birds. It's a kiss my ass affair and they also have a job evaluation plan which must date from the time they built Noah's ark. They have all kinds of schemes which they won't do away with because it allows them to divide and conquer. That's why they're so ferociously opposed to granting any kind of union security.

Johnson:
Their policy, then, is to urge workers to cut each other's throats if they want to be successful in the company?

Gonthier:
They have a whole system at United Aircraft which at every phase of your working life puts you in competition with someone else and therefore it's very hard to develop a strong feeling of solidarity, the kind of solidarity that you need to deal with a company like United Aircraft. The whole thing is quite scientific and it works. That's why they stick with it. The merit system went out the window in the vast majority of companies. At one point, after the Second World War, most major companies had some kind of merit system but they all did away with it in the next twenty years except United Aircraft and General Electric, who stuck with it, and both have a very bad reputation as being solidly anti-union companies. The bible of the United Aircraft personnel advisors — they're supposed to be industrial relations counsellors — is a book entitled "How to meet the challenge of the Union Organizer", and another book they use is called "Union-Free Management".

Johnson:
So they tend to be a very paternalistic type management?

Gonthier:
They are the great white fathers and that's what gets on people's nerves. Nothing is really conceded on merit and yet the merit system is there because it allows them to pick and choose and divide. While you waste your time competing with each other you forget the fact that the policy of the company is the cause of all the problems. That's what you have to bring in line. So we identified nine main issues and we decided to take strike action on these issues. Four of these issues were for negotiation purposes but we had five solid issues that we were determined to win. We had to win these issues if we wanted to get more respect and dignity for the workers.

Johnson:
What were those demands?

Gonthier:
Well, we wanted union security. We wanted the minimum, which is the Rand formula, and to us it was only a question of democracy. If you get services you should pay for the services you get; if you get benefits you should pay the bill.

Johnson:
This manifests itself in the form of a compulsory dues checkoff whether a person belongs to the union or not.

Gonthier:
You don't have to be a member of the union but you have to share the expenses that were incurred to obtain the benefits that you have by being an employee of the company. Another very profound reason

for wanting the Rand formula was that once the majority of a group have chosen to have an organization to represent them, then, in a democracy, the majority rules and the individual choice of the employees in that company that don't want to belong to that organization is to go to work somewhere else. There is nothing stopping people from going to work at a place where there is no union. Another demand was a description of the hours of work and a firm agreement that the work schedules would not be modified without mutual consent. What we were aiming at with this demand, and another closely linked demand of voluntary overtime, was to stop the company from changing the work schedule as they wished and deciding that on a certain day such a department would work on a twelve hour basis and from then on you would work from seven to seven, therefore making overtime compulsory for everybody, and this might last for several months, twelve hours a day seven days a week. And this was happening much too often in that plant to let it go by. We also wanted a cost of living formula. When we negotiated the wage clause we told the company that their monetary offer was satisfactory to us as long as they gave us this cost of living clause, this escalator clause. The formula we were willing to negotiate was not the latest one, it was the previous one which was one cent per $4/10$ of a point augmentation in the consumer price index. This was denied and today they have problems recruiting personnel. Anyway, that's another story. As the strike wore on, of course, other demands arose such as the re-instatement of André Choquette, an employee who had been fired from the company. After the occupation of the plant, yet another set of problems had to be dealt with.

Johnson:
How many men supported the strike at the beginning and how many were opposed?

Gonthier:
Well, the strike vote, which nowadays is only a negotiating mechanism, was ninety-seven per cent in favour of giving the bargaining committee the mandate to declare a strike at the most favourable time. At the time of the first rejection of the company's offer, which was on December 9, 1973, we had over seventy per cent of the membership at the meeting. We had over nineteen hundred people in the hall. Eighty-nine per cent voted in favour of rejecting the company offer. This was the vote which really gave us the mandate to go on strike at the most suitable time. We actually went on strike one month later on January 9 retroactive to January 7 because we were locked out of the company on the morning of January 7. Six weeks later we negotiated again and the company really believed that everybody was going back to work. They had thanked everybody who had done their share during the

previous six weeks and had made the plant ready for our return. We had a membership meeting on the Sunday and they had expected by Monday morning that everybody would be coming back to work. So we had the meeting and presented an amended offer and again we had quite a turnout of the membership, and eighty-four per cent of the people present voted to stay on strike. Of course, we had our defectors even at this early stage, but they were very few and far between. It's also important to remember that we had some three hundred employees who were not members of the union and therefore we could expect as many as three hundred people right from the start that might break ranks and go through the picket lines. But we have to admit that even among those who were not part of the union, many stayed out for the duration of the strike. They refused to go back in because there was a strike on and even though they were not members of the union, they agreed with what we were doing and they stayed out. They told us that they didn't become members of the union because they didn't believe in unionism as such, but they supported the strike in their own ways. Anyway, in the first six months we didn't lose more than two hundred and fifty of our guys. At that point, on July 29, 1974, the Vice-President, Mr. Norris, in Hartford, declared that the strike was over and that the company was re-opening the hiring office and that anybody who didn't go back to work then would never work again at United Aircraft. And also at that point the company sent the foremen and general foremen and even workers on the road to talk to the strikers at home. And they knew the weaknesses of particular workers. A foreman might know that one of his employees liked to drink gin so he would bring along a flask of gin and would start to discuss his life at United Aircraft and try to persuade him to go back. Unfortunately, they were quite successful, using these tactics, in luring back a good five or six hundred employees.

Johnson:
That many? With promises of better jobs or promotions?

Gonthier:
Of course. Or even with a very simple promise of a *job!* Because at that point it was easy to create a panic in a worker's mind, but god-dammit I'll never understand some of these guys. You could create panic in the mind of a guy without a trade or a guy who is not well-educated but why in a guy who would not have any trouble finding a good job even if the plant closed down? Among those guys who went back to work a good many were in the lower scale of wages and they were very often the guys without a trade, the crib attendants, the store attendant, the guy who can be easily replaced. And that's the guy you can really attack and convince or even intimidate. But they were also successful in luring back guys who did have a trade. We do have to make some distinctions though. We have some trades in that plant

that are peculiar to United Aircraft like a Quality Review inspector, for example. He may find a similar job somewhere else but it will never attain the importance it has at United Aircraft. The only place that he might find a job is at another aircraft plant. As I said before, some of the trades there are peculiar to United Aircraft so I can understand some of the older guys being lured back to work on a promise or just the need for a job. But it got to the point where the company was really waging psychological warfare against the workers who remained on strike. And that's exactly what it was. I've been laughed at sometimes for saying that but it's true.

Johnson:
Well, how would you describe the management at United Aircraft, their mentality, the kind of tactics they used?

Gonthier:
They're so backward that, as I've said many times before, they don't belong to the human race. To them, a worker is the most expendable part of a machine, the easiest one to replace, and the only time they show any interest in a worker is when he's not there. You become important when you go on strike, but when you're in the plant you are only part of the machinery. You're only a number. One thing that the strike forced them to change was the punch clock system. There is no longer any punch clock at United Aircraft. Now they "trust" the workers. They watch the workers like they were dogs but they trust them. Before the strike they had a system that was called the short interval system which is actually a very good system in itself. It's designed to find the shortest distance between Point A and Point B and if there is an obstacle in between, you arrange the area so that the obstacle is not there any longer, so you don't lose time going around. But when this system is used to put pressure on the worker to produce more work, you're falsifying the aims of the system and then it becomes inhuman. And when you convince yourself that a hundred per cent is not good enough anymore and that you have to produce a hundred and thirty per cent, then you're really screwing yourself. And in an aircraft engine plant, where precision and perfection is the thing to be obtained, you can't have mass production and you can't have people working under pressure with the tolerances that they have to maintain. The quality of the work over there is fantastic and it has to be that way because when an engine stops up there you don't just pull over to the curb and look at it and find out what's wrong. You have a very long way to go before you reach the curb.

Johnson:
There was a lack of consideration or respect for the workers, then?

Gonthier:
A total lack of consideration or respect. The tactics used ranged from sending letters and making phone calls to personal visits and cajoling and when that didn't work to actual threats and intimidation.

Johnson:
Physical threats or loss of job?

Gonthier:
The loss of job, which can be much worse psychologically than any physical threats. A guy who is past forty years of age is easiest to work on. They were very scientific about it. They told them to start with the men over fifty years of age because these men are less likely to find a job, a suitable job, if the place closed down. So this thing was really planned and they conducted this harrassment in a very scientific manner. And it was effective to a certain extent. The sad part about it is that they succeeded in convincing a large number of people.

Johnson:
How did you feel about the role of the union throughout the strike?

Gonthier:
Well, our union, I'll make a general statement here, is the best in the world. The United Autoworkers is really the kind of union that I'm glad to be part of and I'm proud to have been an officer of the union at that time. We had problems with some individuals but the union as an organization was simply fantastic. The decisions were taken here and the International went along with what we had decided. And nobody ran interference. It might have been tried at a higher level but I've never felt any pressure on me and I have to admit that I played the key role in the strike, along with my fellow officers.

Johnson:
Would you have done anything differently if you were starting all over again from square one?

Gonthier:
Well, your learn from your mistakes but I feel that we didn't make that many mistakes. You know, it made me laugh, because I went to talk to students in universities and CEGEPS and one of the questions that was popped at me many times was, "what's your strategy?". You can't talk of strategy during a strike. A strike is a series of actions and reactions. You have to be able to react to the actions of the other party and you have to make the right decisions all the time. And they are spot decisions. You can't always put off decisions until tomorrow because tomorrow might be too late. Sometimes decisions have to be made on the spur of the moment. You have to be on your toes and wide awake. Would I do anything different from square one? Yes,

I would. We would do our damn best to stay in the plant if the company hadn't changed its mind about using scabs.

Johnson:
You mean an occupation of the plant?

Gonthier:
Yes, but totally. You don't just walk out. You stay in the plant.

Johnson:
And have rotating shifts come in to maintain a presence in the plant?

Gonthier:
If possible, but the first thing that a company is going to do is lock the door on that incoming shift so you won't have any relief. But I would do my damndest to persuade my people to stay in there.

Johnson:
Why? Because you think that it's important that no work be done in the plant, that the workers have control of the machinery?

Gonthier:
Of course, the mere fact of keeping the door open and seeing people walking through the plant gates has a bad influence on striking workers. You allow the psychological warfare to start the minute you walk out of that plant and even if you have a picket line the laws of the land order you to allow people to go through that picket line. You can annoy them if you want, to a certain extent, but they are still going to cross at some point. And at some point you're going to have people in that plant. And having people in the plant other than the men who usually work there starts the process of psychological warfare that is bound to have an effect on the striking workers.

Johnson:
The traditional picket line approach is becoming less effective in certain situations.

Gonthier:
Of course. When a company decides to use scabs your picket line is losing significance because the minute you have people working in the plant all the company has to say and repeat time and again, just like United Aircraft did, is that they are producing, that the strike is not hurting them, and this works on a certain part of your membership. And this is the part that will weaken, and if this part weakens another part of your membership will also start asking themselves questions. And when this ball starts rolling it is a very hard process to stop or reverse.

Johnson:
Do you think the law favours management in strike situations?

Gonthier:
Definitely. The laws of the land are stacked in favour of business. You know, I was listening once to a labour lawyer at a course I took on a definition of the labour code, just a simple definition used in the labour code. He was talking at first about the labour code in general and he told us that at one point we had labour relations which might be described as savage. What he meant was that at one time people sat together and when they had enough problems they would walk out to the parking lot and they would tell the employer that they would walk back if problems A, B and C were solved. Then you got results because you took the employer by surprise and he had to settle the problems if he wanted any production to continue. But that was working too well for workers. They had to create a mechanism whereby the employers would be warned in advance that the strike was coming so they could take steps to combat that strike. Either by stockpiling enough orders to service their customers during the strike or by diverting work elsewhere. They had to find a mechanism to forewarn the employer of labour problems and in came the labour code. That was supposed to "civilize" labour relations but by doing this a monkey wrench was thrown in the works and it doesn't work so well for the worker any more. Ultimately, the labour code benefits management, and the introduction of injunctions in the labour relations field was another major factor that destroyed the efficiency of a strike. Once you start fighting your strike in the courtrooms then you're not on the picket line or in the union hall and your benefit to the membership is nullified.

Johnson:
Very few judges are from the working class. This fact certainly doesn't help workers in any confrontation with management.

Gonthier:
Of course. But you can't throw too many stones at the judges themselves. They are individuals who were born and raised in this system. They went to school to learn the mechanisms of the law and when they became judges they had to apply that law. But they have a whole philosophy which reflects a certain view of life. A view of life which tends to support management. When you are raised in the law and order philosophy you tend to ignore certain things. You see the worker who will not respect an injunction as taking the law into his own hands. To them, this is not law and order any more, it is jungle law. But they do not have to assess whether or not the law that is being invoked is just. The only thing they have to assess is that the law is there and it has to be respected just like any other law.

Johnson:
And the laws are not generally created to favour the working class.

Gonthier:

Definitely not! We have the bad habit of putting in parliament the kind of people that will not pass favourable laws. The traditional parties are financed by big business and you know that a dog never bites the hand that feeds him. And when you are elected to parliament the laws you pass, with the help of the powerful lobby that exists, tend to be the kind of laws that business can live with.

Johnson:

How did you feel about the government's reaction to the strike and the way that they dealt with the situation?

Gonthier:

Well, I think that our government revealed its true character in this situation. Mr. Bourassa (Provincial Prime Minister) is a weakling of the worst sort. The only guy who was really sincere with us and would have done something was Cournoyer (Minister of Labour). But as you remember Cournoyer was removed from the labour department during our strike.

Johnson:

Bourassa's sympathies were with the management?

Gonthier:

He didn't have any choice. He got his orders. He doesn't run fuck all. He's being told what to do. I expressed my disenchantment to him in his office when we met him.

Johnson:

He's being told by whom, Jean? Who is telling him what to do?

Gonthier:

The Liberal caucus, and I don't mean by that the caucus of ministers. The tinkers of the party who are not elected to the House but who are in the background all the time. They are the ones who run the party.

Johnson:

And they represent business interests?

Gonthier:

Definitely. And at this time I would name Jean Lesage (lawyer and former Prime minister) as being one of the guys who retains a great deal of power in that party. And if you look at Jean Lesage today you will see that he doesn't represent any workers. He's on the board of directors of several companies. That kind of people really run the province. Bourassa is only a puppet.

Johnson:

Has this strike radicalized many workers or pushed them into taking a more critical view of the corporations and society?

Gonthier:
Oh yes, it made many workers change their ideas. Some of them, who admitted at the general membership meeting that they had voted Liberal at the last election, told us that they would never vote Liberal again. I think many of our workers saw the light. I won't tell you that these workers would go to war against the government tomorrow but the situation made workers realize that they are "only workers". I've always said that union action or union activities conducted to the hilt awakens workers to political realities. When you get involved in union activities you quickly discover that you are in a highly political situation because at the start of every problem you find a law and when you talk about law you're talking about parliament and when you talk about parliament you talk about politics and you come to realize that if the laws aren't good, and if the people that you put there are not willing to change the laws and make them more palatable to the workers, then you have to change the people in parliament or begin to think of alternatives to the power that exists.

Johnson:
How did you feel about the public reaction to the strike? Some people I've spoken to were almost hysterical in their opposition to the strike.

Gonthier:
Oh yes. Well, you take, for example, all those scabs. And when I talk about scabs I'm talking about those who broke ranks and went back to work as well as those that the company hired. And the families and friends of those people. It represents a lot of people who were bad-mouthing the strike. I can't say that we had a hundred per cent of public opinion behind us, but the vast majority of public opinion supported us. I can vouch for this having participated on so many open line programs where you got maybe two or three of those hysterical people that you talk about who accused us of everything under the sun.

Johnson:
What about the press?

Gonthier:
The vast majority of the journalists were okay with us, but there were a few who were headline mongers. We told them that we didn't like the way that they were doing their work. We are not judges of journalistic work but very often we asked the journalists involved if their job was to inform people or to stir them up with sensational headlines.

Johnson:
What has happened to the workers who decided to occupy the plant and went to jail for it? What's their position now?

Gonthier:

Well, they wanted to engage in a very significant action which would entering and causing damage to the property of the company. There is still one charge pending which is the one about the hostages, and it is due to come up on March 1. The crown will decide when the trial will take place and who they will proceed against. Then we have to go to arbitration with their case before they can return to United Aircraft.

Johnson:

These people felt that, at that time, they had no other alternative but to occupy the plant?

Gonthier:

Well, they wanted to engage in a very significant action which would bring the conflict into the limelight once more. And they definitely succeeded.

Johnson:

So action of this nature is sometimes the only way that you can draw attention to the problem?

Gonthier:

The people that we were aiming at with this action, I say we because I have to feel a part of it even though I was not with the group, was the government, not the company. We had known for some time that there was nothing we could do with this company, that any settlement would have to be imposed on them. And if Bourassa had been the leader that he claims to be he would have imposed a settlement on them just like he passed a law, Bill 29 and 30, to supposedly contain the construction workers' unions. He should have passed a law against United Aircraft just to prove to those companies that might be tempted to go the United Aircraft route that this would not be tolerated in Québec. And the whole scheme of labour relations would have been better off if he had done so because any crazy company that would have been tempted to use the tactics that United Aircraft had used on us would have had to think twice.

Johnson:

So you think that the government acted cowardly and did not really concern themselves with the long term interests of the workers and the people of Quebec?

Gonthier:

You're putting it very mildly. I have much stronger words for Mr. Bourassa's behaviour which are not fit for publication.

A number of issues raised in this interview could not be discussed because of pending court cases.

Working in an Office

by Michael Katzemba

Canadians are continually bombarded by media coverage of various forms of labour unrest and dissatisfaction. The Prime Minister warns that Canadians are second only to the Italians in the total number of man hours lost in strikes. This type of action, we are told, is a contributing factor to inflation (we have only ourselves to blame!) and dire economic forecasts abound. The notion of a passive labour force has completely disappeared and has instead been replaced by the spectre of a highly powerful and politicized labour force, conscious of its position and constantly attentive to any encroachments made against its status.

The above stereotype, however, cannot be applied to all areas of the work force. The image of the white collar worker has remained intact. The picture of caution, conservatism and willing compliance still prevails. Juxtaposed to the militancy of the blue collar work force, it is a passive and compromising group of seemingly distinct individuals, each independent and conscious of his particular position, able to articulate and rationalize a philosophy of self-interest. Through the use of slick advertising and media-manipulation techniques, white collar work still holds the trappings of respect and deference that it did decades ago. Despite the fact that the economic and social gains made by unionized labour have far outstripped that of the white collar work force, success, as promoted by education, media and myth, can still be equated with white collar lifestyles and situations. In an era of technological advance that has rendered almost all tasks meaningless and dull, the idea of the office as being the repository of industrial brainwork continues to endure.

It appears to me that the consequence of this sort of thinking, and the promotion of the qualities and abilities required in this area of work, are a clear reflection of an attitude prevalent in our society; a definite statement as to who is able to administer and for whose benefit society exists. The myths and qualities about people which white collar labour seems to propagate, can only have negative connotations for a society in which harmony is being touted as an ideal. The myths

---

Mike Katzemba works as a production expediter for a Montréal firm.

and traditional wisdom through which society is operated, in order to be successful, must have an affect upon the way in which people regard each other and carry out their daily relations with one another.

In the following article, I wish to expose some of the myths and operational thinking regarding individuals involved in white collar work, and show how this encourages and promotes relations amongst people based upon authoritarian precepts. This, in turn, can only be a reflection of the social premise that the worth of one's fellow man is judged by his use value in attaining certain imposed goals. The generalizations which I tend to make are based upon subjective analysis of given situations, while my theoretical readings on the subject have been minimal. Although my observations may be disproved by isolated examples and instances, I believe that, in general, the contacts and business situations encountered in my work tend to substantiate my opinions. In any case, the frustrations and responses articulated by my fellow workers form the basis of this article.

If I had to describe the basic ingredient in the psychology of the office, fear would be the first which would come to mind. The fear of getting into "trouble", the fear of not appearing competent or capable in the eyes of superiors or peers is probably the motivating factor responsible for the smooth operation of the office environment. Indeed, when one understands the manner in which most offices are set up, and the competitive aspect which this setup engenders, it becomes totally logical that fear should be the catalyst which makes office dynamics operate. This requires an explanation.

Ideally, the nature of office work should provide the employee with a broad overview of the operations of the enterprise. Through the use of the data at hand, the functions and problems involved in the enterprise would become apparent to the clerical worker; he could apply creative thought and imagination in order to overcome specific problems. During the early years of the industrial revolution, this was indeed the case. Office procedures were kept to a minimum and the relatively small numbers of office employees were exposed to a wide range of functions and information. The clerical staff worked in close contact with plant personnel as well as with owners and managers, and their insight and knowledge of the enterprise was indispensable to its proper operation. However, the growing complexity of all aspects of industrial output resulted in the increase of office procedures and techniques. Development of new methods of accounting, planning, marketing, salesmanship, etc., resulted in the formation of independent departments manned by specialists in each one, thereby narrowing the perspective of the employees involved. The net result we see in the form of the office hack, sitting at a desk adding up rows of indistinguishable figures on an electric calculator.

This loss of a total overview of the function of the industry is central to understanding the position of the office employee. The possibility of planning work on a long term basis, and of using particular judgement and the information at one's disposal, is out of the question. The worker is instead tied to a particular specialized task to which he has been assigned and is given just enough information to enable him to carry out that task efficiently. The worker is left without any realistic criteria by which he can judge his work. What becomes measurable is the amount and quality of the paperwork which he has produced. It is at this point where the employee is totally at the mercy of his superior, who does have access to the information by which work can be judged. Not only does the actual work have very little connection to any kind of real production or activity, but the employee, in most cases, must second-guess his boss and seek affirmation so as to ensure that he is indeed performing his task adequately. The position of actual judgement is left up to the superior.

This fear of being judged by criteria of which one has no knowledge leads to heights of absurdity and frustration. I have personally witnessed employees being verbally abused for performing work which no longer needed to be done, but because of lack of information, the same useless task continued to be performed.

Such a position serves the purpose of the direct superior in two principal ways. First, it insures that the bosses' prerogatives will be followed smoothly and without question. It becomes next to impossible to question certain actions when one is not aware of all the facts involved. Secondly, it tends to make the superior seem indispensable to the efficient operation of his department. He himself, and possibly others, will tend to acquire an inflated appraisal of his abilities and intellect when, in fact, he simply has access to more information from which others are barred. Workers then become encouraged to leave the decision-making to "capable" hands, and content themselves with the processing of data.

It is easy to see that from the position in which the employee is placed, that he is totally at the mercy of his superior. If this is not at first apparent, it is made abundantly clear by the attitude of most bosses toward their employees. It becomes very evident "who's the boss". Being in a totally powerful position, the boss is free to vent his emotions upon his inferiors. It is quite normal to see the boss throw minor temper tantrums and verbally abuse those around him, such as secretaries and clerks. Whether it be an obvious disdainful attitude, or one refined by some university course in industrial manipulation, the condescending presence of authority is painfully present in the office setting. The employee, in any case, is left with the grim choice of swallowing his pride and putting up with some minor assault against his personality, or retaliating in anger and facing dismissal. As always, the naked exercise of power is acutely visible.

The fear of getting into trouble has also another aspect in the office psychology. The safety valve which enables office brass to avert rebellion from the frustration suffered by the staff is the promise of promotion to those jobs where the exercise of judgement is permissible.

It is therefore important for the employee to appear to be as competent as possible, to be "on the ball". This is best accomplished by second-guessing the boss as to what is the most profitable and constructive task to be engaged in, vis-à-vis his particular requirements. To be out of tune with those requirements means you have a difficult time "catching on" to what is happening around you. This, of course, exposes the individual to the scrutiny of higher authority in that he has not conformed to group operational thinking and psychology, rendering him isolated and non-functional. To incur the wrath of higher authority in this manner renders one's chances of promotion next to nil. It is this tool which is the most powerful in the bosses' arsenal for the pacification of their employees. This aura of fear becomes ingested to the point where the crude exercise of authority is no longer needed. Instead the employees will second-guess themselves into complete subservience, and internalize a code of behaviour which makes them capable of performing any duty, no matter how mundane or stupid. Orders no longer have to be given. A hint or clue will ensure their accomplishment.

For those unfamiliar with the office setting perhaps what has been expressed above may appear to be an exaggeration and an expression of the paranoia of its author. When removed from a work situation one would be impressed by the forceful and articulate expression of opinion of a group of office workers. There would appear to exist a state of healthy disagreement on almost any topic. In the office situation, this hypothesis undergoes radical transformation. One is instead confronted by a definite streamlining of opinion. Each individual, especially in the presence of superiors, becomes acutely aware of his position in the group consensus. Forceful opinions at the beginning of a discussion become more modified as time develops until finally, it will usually blend in with the prevailing opinion — usually that of the boss.

At this point, I would like to attempt to describe the effects which the office environment has upon the philosophy and social outlook of the white collar worker. Again I wish to stress that my opinions have been arrived at through participation and observation with my workmates of the office setting. Indeed, the effect which the office environment has had on my own beliefs, when I place them in the perspective of this article, has been considerable. I believe that the manner in which one is forced to make a living becomes the primary activity to the individual. The effect which this has upon his perception of society and fellow men is unmistakable. If our places of work are brutal and dehumanizing, then it would appear difficult to change such a perception of the world around us.

As I have previously tried to describe, the chief factor in the working environment of the office is the total powerlessness of the worker and his complete susceptibility to authority. The lack of any kind of union solidarity, and the competitive relationship with other workers in terms of promotion, makes most office workers hopelessly divided. It also places the individual in a position of being totally dependent on higher authority for the fulfillment of his present needs and future ambitions. The worker is forced to regard his advancement and progress in life on a very individualistic level, and, if necessary, at the expense of others. It also causes the worker to believe that his talents and abilities are superior to those of others, and that it is only a matter of time before those talents are recognized and suitably rewarded.

With the above in mind, the stereotype of the "grey flannel" lifestyle becomes understandable. The conservatism, isolation and compliance of white collar workers as a group, appears to be a logical extension of their work environment. The fear which I have encountered amongst office workers, of any kind of change in the system of power as it exists, is an indication of the extent to which their personal well-being is tied to authority. During a recent occupation of their plant by striking United Aircraft workers, the reaction of most of my office co-workers was a mixture of hatred and revulsion. The fact that authority had been subverted and private property ignored brought an almost hysterical reaction. The news that many of the strikers had been physically abused by police officers brought general agreement that those hoodlums had received their just rewards.

As this is being written the plant personnel of the enterprise where I am employed are conducting a strike which is in its sixth week. The reaction of the office workers has been most interesting and tends to substantiate my previous comments. A number of office employees, including myself, who appear to be peripheral to the basic functioning of the enterprise, have been temporarily laid off. Since there has been no decrease in the amount of work carried out in the office, those who have remained have had to double up and perform the tasks of those who have been turfed out. It appears obvious that this is simply a way for the company to squeeze more work out of the employees while saving money on a reduced payroll.

The anger and frustration which one would expect the office workers to feel at this outrage is not directed at management, but instead at the plant union. There is almost universal agreement amongst the office staff that management, with their backs to the wall due to the irresponsible blackmailing of the union, acted in the only possible way by cutting costs and piling more work on the remaining employees. The acceptance and rationalization of this increased exploitation and job insecurity, shows the lengths to which office workers have been trained to accept authority and arbitrary decisions. There appears to be no thought or possibility of a collective confrontation of management by the office staff in the face of such obvious exploitation.

The fact that the unionized workforce in the plant will receive a much larger pay increase than any of the office staff, does not seem to enhance the image of collective action amongst my co-workers. The idea of collective action seems to be completely anathema to their belief that through individual merit and striving, they will individually overcome their present lot.

Finally, I believe that among many of my co-workers, there is a basic belief that they form a caste apart from the unionized plant personnel. The necessity of blue collar workers to band together is seen as a replacement for individual talent and merit. It is said that all they must perform is their physical labour, that they have no responsibility, whereas office workers must answer for any mistakes which may occur in our work. Many in the office would prefer not to mix with the shop personnel because of a lack of culture and appropriate mannerisms.

Whether the present demeaning state of white collar work can remain unchanged in the future is questionable. The grim reality of spending ones life in a dead end job in an industrial wasteland is replacing the Horatio Alger myth of rising through corporate echelons through one's merit and ability. The philosophy of laissez faire individualism is gradually becoming impossible to rationalize and maintain in the face of daily work experiences.

At present, there appears to me to be certain identifiable social phenomena which could prevent the historically passive role of white collar psychology from enduring.

Among the new generation of white collar workers the expectations derived from exposure to higher education and cultural changes are creating real dissatisfaction with the stifling institutional thinking of the office world. Beginning in the 1960's, hiring of university educated personnel became a trend among large companies, and university enrollment grew by 50%. Students who flocked to universities to receive B.A.'s, B. Comm.'s, and B.Sc.'s, have in many cases been exposed to ideas and philosophies which are incompatible with the realities of their working environment. Along with increased education, experimentation with more liberated lifestyles or philosophies has had a definite influence in the thinking of young workers. Most find a rude awakening to a grim reality when they enter the office world. In few cases do job challenge and capacity match the educational requirement of that position. It appears that employers are able to demand overeducated people to fill routine jobs simply because there exists a glut of such people on the labour market. For these people, the frustrations caused by a stifling, uncreative job, coupled with their heightened expectations, cause them to critically examine the managerial organization of the work process, and to look towards more humane and non-alienating solutions to the organization of work.

The impact which the women's movement has had on the consciousness of female white collar workers is also evident. Certain issues which have been raised by women's liberation helped female office workers to recognize their inherent disadvantage in the work situation. Most obvious is the issue of unequal pay for equal work. Women seldom receive wages comparable to that of men in the same job classification. In most cases, however, this comparison is difficult to make since most women are segregated into low paying, low status jobs from which men are exempt. Seventy percent of all clerical jobs are occupied by women engaged in routine filing, typing, book-keeping, or jobs requiring little responsibility. For the vast majority of these women, promotion to managerial positions where the exercise of judgement is permissible, will never come about. Women in the office setting are generally not treated as serious participants in the function of the enterprise. The general belief is that most are biding time until they marry and raise families. The married working women are thought to be contributing to the family income for frivolous extras, when in reality it is the wages of the working mother which keeps many Canadian families above the poverty level. These beliefs are translated into a rather paternalistic and condescending attitude by male workers toward their female counterparts. In most offices where I have worked, there existed a commonly held male belief that their female co-workers were cute but rather naive and superficial office furnishings, not really capable of rational decision making.

To combat this situation, working women have begun to organize. Pressure has been applied to government bodies in order to prevent discrimination in hiring practices and salary scales. Public attention has been awakened to groups of women taking legal action against individual companies for discriminatory practices. In Montreal, an organization of working women called Rank & File has recently been formed to combat unfair employment practices. Unionized female workers in the public sector have established committees "Condition Feminin" to locate discrimination within collective agreements and to pressure union negotiators to make demands in collective agreements for such things as day care centres, maternity benefits, etc.

This type of organizing, although in its embryonic stages, is a clear indication that women will no longer remain passive to the inferior status which has been accorded to them at work and in society at large.

Finally, I believe that recent unionization and militancy of white collar workers within the public sector can only act as a guideline for employees in the private sector. It has become obvious that nurses, postal employees, teachers, Hydro workers and municipal workers and other unionized white collar workers have been better protected against the ravages of inflation and job insecurity than workers who have had to individually battle for their interests against powerful employers. The fact that militant action has been taken by workers with professional and semi-professional training can only enhance the idea of such action in the minds of office workers. Especially in Québec, white collar workers in the public sector have proven to be conscious of their solidarity with blue collar workers, as witnessed by their vigorous participation in the May, 1972 General Strike, and the present Common Front confrontation of government employees with their employer.

In the examples I have cited, formation of white collar trade unions and corresponding militancy is not necessarily a sign of radical political transformation of these workers. But given the history and collective psychology of workers traditionally associated with this area of work, the recognition of the fact that only collective action, as opposed to individual striving, is capable of adequately defending their interests, can only be regarded as a progressive step in the identification of their social position and development of a political consciousness.

Just Working

by Gary Jewell

It has always astonished me: the stereotype so many radical intellectuals have of the 'working class'. That these are the very group of people the middle class radical spends so much time speaking about, or even in the name of, yet knows so little about, is a large part of the irony. Not that every intellectual still pictures the working class as a shambling, lantern-jawed Irishman. Nor a muscled, vacant-eyed Apollo from some Socialist Realism mural.

No, the present *mythology* is far more insidious. Physical type is no longer the primary touch-stone. What today marks the difference between a worker and a middle class intellectual is *pure knowledge*. The worker has only gut grievances. The middle class radical *knows*. And therefore the logical conclusion: any worker who has radical knowledge, must be an apostate or a middle class *expatriate* in disguise.

I think it was this prejudice — even more so than capitalist exploitation — that made me *consciously* aware that I was working class.

To begin with, I did not pursue formal education, although I could have. Finishing high school, I could read and write *and did so*. If I wished to crack a primer on Marx or Bakunin, it was within my ability and I did so. I wasn't typical, but I met a lot of working guys who did so too. Later, though, when I first started associating with radical intellectuals, I was a bit chagrined. If ever I let slip a little working class prejudice, especially if it were in conjunction with a radical analysis, the rejoinder was always so swift:

"Oh, come on, you're middle class. You've been to University!"

It was such insults that helped resolve certain antipathies building up in me since I was in my teens. The arrogance in the presumption that anyone with a bit of radical knowledge was *ergo* middle class or a University product, crystalized my class consciousness.

A consciousness made all the more bitter because so many fellow workers share the prejudice, though in reverse fashion.

Gary Jewell works as a warehouseman in Toronto and is the editor of the Industrial Defence Bulletin.

Perhaps this is too tendentious. So be it. For it is no small gripe to a lot of radical workers — and there are more around than one would usually suspect — this condescension and little suppressed shock that someone could be radicalized outside the campus in North America and yet have all the signs of a WASP.

I am not representative of the North American work force, nor the Canadian worker. Yet it might be of interest to the reader how just one worker became radicalized. And how he presently fits into the broad mosaic of the working class in Canada today.

My mother's family were French and Alsatian Québecois who migrated west at the turn of the century, down into Minnesota. By the 1920's they had reached California. My father's people were English, Scottish, Irish, Welsh, German, Dutch and Cherokee Indian: farmers that began drifting into California in the 1880's, riding on the very railroads that had bankrupted their farms in Illinois and Missouri. A great-great-grandfather was a Eugene V. Debs — Socialist; he voted Socialist until his death in the 1930's. The skeleton in the family closet.

My two grandfathers and one step-grandfather were a house painter, a factory guard, a welder, carpenter and plumber. None were especially class conscious. But as a kid, listening to family conversations when they turned to reminiscences of the Depression, I remember them always speaking of a man called "pig Hoover". Never Herbert Hoover, nor President Hoover; always "pig Hoover".

You may have seen over the last few years a popular T.V. situation comedy, "All in the Family" — whose arch hero/villain, Archie Bunker, is a supposed pastiche of the American workingman. Yet the dialogue is ridiculously petite-bourgeois in origin, and not the kind of reactionary materialism which does infect the working class. A blue collar loading dock foreman, Bunker and his prejudices are put to scorn weekly. Each episode begins with he and *the wife* at the piano singing, "...we could use a man like Herbert Hoover again." Bullshit. That is not the view of a worker who went through the early Thirties with Hoover at the helm, not even a worker who later voted for Eisenhower or Nixon. It is a merchant or government service attitude, not that of an industrial worker... no matter how degenerated.

My father, coming from a poor and broken home, was shaped into a military cast by the war. The day after Pearl Harbor, Monday morning, December 8, 1941, he enlisted, age 17. As a paratrooper he saw action in North Africa, Sicily, Italy, Holland and Germany, was wounded twice and decorated with a Bronze Star for bravery. Demobilized and in need of a job in 1945, he joined the police force, working from motorcycle cop to the youngest sergeant and then lieutenant in the nation's crack gestapo, the Los Angeles Police Department.

A small delicate girl in her teens, my mother worked in a defense plant making fighter planes. War's end, she married and raised children. Her periodic waitressing jobs bolstered the always overstretched family credit accounts.

We lived in an upper working class tract of homes in Whittier, California, where acres of orange trees had made way before the developer's bulldozers. Two blocks away was a corner grocery store and soda fountain: NIXON'S. Near it was the Nixon family home, a modest two-storey affair soon to be torn down and replaced by a shopping plaza. Richard Nixon had just become vice president; his nephew I knew slightly: once I remember stuffing firecrackers into peaches with him, exploding them in mid-air. Just recently I heard of him again, in connection with the post-Watergate investigations: seems he became a front man and pimp for the globe-trotting financier Vesco.

When the Nixons' sold out and moved on to better things, Donald Nixon — Dick's brother — built a luxurious two-level super market near the old Quaker Church in East Whittier, and down the road a hamburger stand. No common fast-food joint was this. Emblazoned in neon was NIXONBURGERS. A circular drive led to roofed carports, customers connected to the grill by way of intercoms. Soon, a 'young thing' in a very short skirt would dash out to the car with a tray of burgers, fries and malts; the tray attached to the car by a clip. Then you'd dig into those juicy Nixonburgers!

I always wondered how they traded that crummy corner store for all this. I supposed that Dick, what with his vice presidential salary, loaned the money to family businessman Donald. It was only in that crescendo that led to Watergate that the truth came out. Howard Hughes had set up a fraudulent charity organization as a tax dodge, but the IRS turned down his application for a tax exemption. Hughes then gave Donald Nixon $200,000 as a personal gift to build the hamburger stand. Lo and behold, decision reversed, Hughes was granted the tax exemption.

Dick did make sure though that the stand changed its name to Whirleyburgers.

When I was twelve, my father, on the verge of bankruptcy from a new house he could not afford, died suddenly. My mother remarried a sergeant in the U.S. Army artillery. He soon transfered back into his old specialty, military criminal police, and was sent to a post in West Germany. As the Berlin and Cuban Crises were raging, our family was not allowed to accompany him, but my stepfather paid our way over himself and lodged us in an apartment in a German working class district. My new buddies were 14 year old kids already apprenticed to a trade and working full time — and for no wages at that, just a

133

stipend for mother and a couple of Marks for beers. To my astonishment, most of my fellow carousers at the rifleman's club came from social democratic families (I had been expecting Nazis). 'Socialists!' And me come but lately of Orange County, California; home of the John Birch Society and the Minutemen.

I rather quickly learned just what a U.S. occupation looks like to the common man abroad. Passing a U.S. base one night with a German comrade, we were accosted by two drunken American soldiers. These were 18 or 19 year old kids from places like Shit Creek Georgia, who now found themselves in the dog-eat-dog world of the U.S. paratroops. Fifty or so miles away Russian tank forces were poised in that East German bulge deep into West Germany near Frankfurt. These kids, backed by tactical nuclear weapons (which differentiate neither friend nor foe), were to be the suicide troops who held the Russians (kids from Shitski Krik, Volga Valley) just long enough for the U.S. to airlift forces to France and make a last stand (no wonder de Gaulle kicked the U.S. out).

These punks were driven to sheer bestiality by their sadistic sergeants and officers. Little surprise that on payday they went berserk in the streets of that German Rhineland city. Rape, murder, brutal assault and robbery were so common it didn't seem the U.S. Army was capable of anything more. As I was to learn as the pair of drunken troopers began to viciously kick us in that cobblestone alley.

At fifteen I became quite depressed and began to write and also to read Kafka and Borchert and even more sombre works. Out of desperation I turned to Jack London adventure novels to bolster my manhood. I soon became adept at sneaking off on week-ends to freeze on the river banks and in abandoned cellars with old wino bums, listening to their stories of the sea, fights with the Gestapo, and of punishment battalions on the Russian front.

Learning in an encyclopedia that my hero Jack London was a Socialist, I was shocked. I found an excerpt from *The Iron Heel,* his 1907 prophesy of fascism in America and the socialist underground battling it. Impressed, I got more books from the libraries on the military base and Defense Department High School I attended: selections from Karl Marx, Harrington's *The Other America,* history of the Anarchists, the 1877 Railroad Riots. I soon announced that I was a revolutionary socialist and dialectical materialist (of all things). I was attending an Air Force school, which also numbered a score of colonels' and generals' sons and daughters, some driving sports cars to the grounds. I came each day on an Army bus from across the river with the brood of paratrooper sergeants, mostly southern "white trash" and "niggers". I must have appeared mighty strange among them, the stern-faced Red who dressed and looked like a Kraut.

Talking socialism and against U.S. Imperialism was somewhat risky. Especially when Kennedy was shot and I informed Germans and Americans alike that the "fascists" got him, only to have the *Stars and Stripes* newspaper reveal the assassin as a "marxist". There are times when one lives dangerously.

At seventeen I took a job as a handy-man, then left home. I wound up back in the U.S., broke, a punk kid who couldn't even buy a legal piss-water beer (after the oceans of Bier in Germany). Thus started my life-long hate relation with the inanity of American society. A culture which keeps a boy in a fantasy cocoon until he is 18, then sends him into a factory or to Vietnam to sweat or bleed out his innocence in one great visceral blow. It is a society which systematically rapes its youth and cripples its soul.

For the next eight years I wandered as in an obsessive dream all over North America, Europe, and Asia. Joys there were a few of, and comradeship. But mostly I remember the pains and fears, the rupturing jobs and degrading conditions, the hungers and sicknesses; the fights and escapes from police, smuggled borders, threats of death from petty criminals and bandits. And everywhere the relentless authority of the State. I was forced to seek my manhood alone, unaided, and under constant attack. It was, as Gorki called it, "my university".

On periodic returns to the U.S. I usually got in on Vietnam protest marches, and for some damn reason I always found myself in the very section of the march where the police or the Nazis or the Cuban *gusanos* attacked. I saw a lot of action. Afterwards, the few radical meetings I attended always alienated me. I'd read Marx and Guevara, but what was this strange language they were speaking? Only later, finally reading Lenin, Trotsky, Stalin and Mao did I catch on to their specialized trade jargon. It was certainly something I could never use when I had to go back to work the next day at the warehouse.

It was my final trip through south-western Asia and India that forced me to take a new stock. In India particularly, the appalling misery, starvation, disease and seemingly hopeless apathy shocked me to the core. Physically I reached rope's end as well. North of Bombay I came down with dysentery. I just managed to drag myself back across Pakistan, Afghanistan, Iran, and Turkey, shitting my guts bloody enroute. Selling my worthless blood in Greece, I lived on milk and cheese and nursed myself back into a semblance of life.

A few months back in the Unites States, after two labouring jobs and having crossed the Continent twice with a foray into Mexico, I found myself dead broke in Augusta, Georgia. Lining-up morning at the Georgia State Employment Office with young and old Blacks, waiting for some red-necked Georgian contractor to drive by in his pick-up truck and yell over: "You three boys get in the back... Eh, you, son. You wanna work? Get in the front seat. I pay State minimum if you can swing a pick."

When I at last 'escaped' back to California, I took work at a rope factory as a machine operator. I was paid scarcely more than the State minimum wage, and that because I was a male. The women employed there, mostly poor white and Mexican who worked at the more delicate (and excruciatingly nerve-wracking) fine-thread machines, earned less than I. The factory looked like a vignette out of Engel's 1840 Birmingham. The din of spinning machines and whine of synthetic twine was so terrible that we were obliged to wear ear plugs. The company paid no compensation for burst eardrums or inner ear deterioration if it could be proven that even once you left them out. Not that they really helped much: it was pandemonium.

I ran a double (two-sided) 50-foot long loom with 5 feeding reels on each side that produced a 3-4 inch thick plastic rope wound around two massive wooden reels. I was not only running up-and-down the two sides of this machine, but at the same time was expected to keep the bobbins full and running on eight minor spinning looms nearby, all of which took twelve full-bobbins of twine each to produce the heavy 5 plus 5 reels I spliced into the major loom.

It was work for three men, two at speed-up. I did it alone and was under constant harassment, until the day I quit in a rage, for underproduction. We had no safety guards on the machines (I was nearly strangled to death once; another time I was hauled half-way to the ceiling when the rope caught my thumb — I cut myself loose with a knife. Dropping, I almost fell into the massive revolving arms of the machine). We males had no rest breaks except lunch and we had to punch in-and-out on the time clock for that. (By State law, women were given two ten minute rest breaks each shift. With the new "equality" legislation, they'll now join the men).

Now comes the worst horror of all: the factory was a "union" closed shop, organized by the United Steelworkers. The factory manager faithfully remitted a "union" dues check-off from our pay to the Steelworkers local — 40 miles away. At no time did we ever have a steward or ever see a union representative. That is what is known as a "sweetheart contract".

One day reading an 'underground' hippy newspaper, I saw an ad: "Yes, there is a Debs-Thomas Socialist Party". I joined them — a tiny dissident left-wing, called the Debs Caucus, which was fighting the nearly defunct head office in New York City, the latter a morally bankrupt gaggle of pro-Vietnam War renegades under one-time Trotskyite Max Schachtman, who was in cahoots with George Meany and his AFL-CIO red-baiting jackal, J. Lovestone (who, believe it or not, was the 1920's leader of the Communist Party USA who expelled the Trotskyites). But the Debs Caucusers, though pure of heart, were too tame and social democratic for me (I wanted total rupture with the Schacht-manites; it took them five more years) and I drifted around a number of Trotskyite and Maoist organizations. They always wanted me to flog their newspapers at Vietnam protest marches. "Listen," I'd say, "I work as an apprentice machinist down in Orange County. That's Minuteman and Bircher territory. The machine shop is non-union. The guys at work are pissed off with things, but they're pretty conservative. I can't pass this newspaper around the shop. It's all about students protests and the Third World. There's nothing in it about workers."

"It's not time for the workers," the earnest SWP/YSA type would patiently explain to me. "Right now its the students who are in motion. We've got to go where they are. Later, when things are ripe, *the workers will come to us.*"

That's just one reason why I never did join the Marxist-Leninists.

In 1970 I found myself in Toronto visiting a German-American buddy who was dodging the draft. (I fortunately had done a mere 2½ month stint in the military at 18-19, landing a medical discharge a month before I was to be shipped to Vietnam. Otherwise, I might still be on the run and debating "Amnesty"). Aside from work, the primary 'political' thing I remember about 1970 was the War Measures Act in Canada: the hysterical anti-French fascists crawling out of the woodwork, the silence of the "good liberals", the police raid on a Guelph University newspaper which had dared to print the FLQ 'terro-rist' demands, and the fear that went through the exile community when two American war resistors from Montréal were picked up in Toronto by the RCMP. Coupled with the police attacks on the 'Cam-bodia invasion' protest demonstration at the U.S. Consulate in Toronto earlier in May, it gave Canada a much more sinister look and certainly dispelled the Trudeau Mania of the '60's from a lot of starry-eyed middle class student types.

For two years I stuck around Hogtown, crossing into Upper New York State periodically to do factory or shop labour for so many months, then 'retiring' to Toronto on my income (I had not immigrated, so could not work in Canada). These were some pretty rotten jobs, as jobs go. One in particular was in Niagara Falls, N.Y., where I worked in a carbon factory down in the pits — a job mis-organized by the United Mine Workers. My first day there I was given the job no one else wanted. 12-foot long columns of graphite or carbon were lowered by crane into the pits and stood on-end. Sand was then poured in until the rows of columns and entire pits were covered. Underground passages fed gas-fueled flames into the sand and the columns were baked at a tremendous heat. When things cooled down — say to 600 degrees — it was my job to walk out on the red-hot brick walls, perhaps a foot-wide and crumbling with frequent gaps, wearing wooden shoes with broken straps or defective buckles and carrying a shovel and a steel pole. My initial job was to shovel sand off until the tops of the columns were exposed. Then the crane driver dropped a heavy claw down (don't let it hit you, you'll be knocked into the burning sand. If you haven't already fallen unconscious from the heat or a possible gas leak). With the pole you prodded and pushed the claw, which had been repaired one too many times, hoping to fit it snugly about the top of the column. Having succeeded, the crane driver away up at the ceiling and across the pits, yanked-up with all the electrically-induced power of the crane cables. But wait. A long channel runs along the side of the column. This had been re-enforced with wooden pegs to prevent collapse. The wood supports are now char-wood adhering to the column. It must come out, but to pry it out later when the column has been laid on the floor to cool would be a waste of precious man-power. After all, you are standing there with a sharpened pole as the column is surfaced. So dig, boy, pick and scrape as that column barrels past you and don't leave a shred of char, as your job depends on it. Trouble is, the suction caused by the up-doing column ushers forth a belching whirlwind of gas, smoke, hot sand and cinders — directly into your face. You are dying, choking, but faster, get that char out!

After a while, I got a better job. When the columns had been removed, as well as the tons of sand, down at the bottom of the narrow but deep pits a residue of baked carbon, graphite, sand and crushed brick remained, sometimes 3 or 4 feet thick. Down into that terrible heat you go, by regulation with a buddy, but often alone, with a jack-hammer, pick and shovel to blast, pry and shovel it up. Once you've got a good pile, the crane driver, who can't even see you down there but operates on feel alone, lowers a claw-bucket to scoop up your treasure. Just hope that the bucket doesn't come down on you, or that the cable doesn't snap (which the company claims is impossible, but you've seen it happen twice). Or that the bucket doesn't knock one of those loose, heat-fractured cap stones up-top down upon you (you've been hit twice by falling bricks, and so have the other boys. Wasn't there a guy who got killed right before you hired on?). One could go on forever about all the great jobs in that place.

But I want to end this job with the *pitch*. As in 'pitch-black'. The pitch, in a dust form, gets in your pores. Later you shower in hot water and the pores open wider. The pitch digs deeper into the more tender flesh. Pitch burns, like hell-fire. Then you go out into the sun. Open, pitch-burned pores: radiation from the sun jabs in. Your face is in flames. Tough luck, sucker. You are a member of the pampered North American working class, remember?

Later, back in Canada, I managed to get, through some old

socialist contacts, a copy of a strange little newspaper: the *Industrial Worker*. The I.W.W.? Industrial Workers of the World. Hell, are they still alive? Well, it made me laugh, this thin working class rag. Jumbled together were articles written by old duffer Wobs, young factory stiffs, and long-haired street freaks. I put it aside for six months.. kind of amused. But then, dead broke again, I wound up in Rochester N.Y., forced to take a job so lowpaid and so humiliating I couldn't believe it.

It was essentially three jobs: electric assembler, stores handler, and errand boy, all for an electrical fixture showroom. It was a job normally given to a 17 year old kid fresh from school, so dumb or so desperate he wouldn't realize he was doing the job of three men. And me? I was broke, snow was in the air. I begged for the job.

I assembled and wired everything from table lamps to $3,000 crystal chandeliers. These were shown-off in a glittering display room, which I again assembled and wired. At the same time I was expected to keep in order and receive from the shipping-receiving department all the thousands of boxes of lamps and fixtures in storage. Moreover, at the beck and call of the sales manageress and four saleswomen, I rushed up and down the three floors, bringing fixtures to delight the eye of customers, boxing what they purchased and hauling it out to their cars. Most importantly, however, I was to kiss the ass of the owner, his son, all his other relatives, the sales manageress, and to humour the overworked saleswomen.

During this period I lived in a small coffin at the YMCA, which was actually a lonely old men's death home. I busted ass six days a week all winter: take-home pay of $65. Nights I spent eating tins of cold herrings in my luxury suite while watching Nixon and Haldeman and Kissinger on T.V. I wrote to Chicago, saying 'let me join the I.W.W.' I received my union red card in the mail down at the YMCA front desk.

After I was fired from my job, I traveled to Chicago and worked for over a month at union headquarters. I and a lumpen kid from California, Arthur Miller. A startling fellow with long fair hair, grey eyes and Apache Indian cheekbones. Sleeping on cots in the library, fighting off rats, influenza, winos, thieves and dope addicts.. trying to help the Wobblies get the union back on its feet and out there into the factories. They had already fought a few small strikes, and damn, it was worth a try.

Miller had fought a two year IWW free speech fight in San Diego, home of the original Wobbly fight in 1910. He was a hawker for the IWW-unionized *Street Journal* — a muckraker which exposed the mayor and city council. Inside information was coming from the assistant D.A., who wanted his boss' position (and got it). When the bourgeois press finally picked it up, President Nixon's favourite mayor was forced out and a part of the city council indicted on graft charges. But the young Wobs there had it none too easy, especially when the new D.A. sought to cover his past dealings. The fascist Minutemen firebombed the co-op commune, bombed the newspaper truck, and shot down one girl, paralyzing her arm for life. To cap it off, a Portuguese Wobbly and two Chicanos were arrested on the old Criminal Syndicalism law (the law was finally ruled unconstitutional, but the trio were framed on a firebomb charge).

Miller and I went our respective ways, he to California and I back to Toronto. A few weeks later I got word that 19 year old Miller had tried to get a job at a pool filter factory; turned down, he talked to a few workers going out, heard their gripes and invited them all to meet him at the United Farmworkers Hall after quitting time. He signed the whole factory up IWW and they (prematurely) walked out on strike. It ended with a court injunction, police raids on the picket line and jailings, plus the Teamsters trying to muscle in (we lost, but we did beat out the Teamsters). While it was going, it was some show: the first large IWW strike in basic industry since the Cleveland metal shops in the 1930's.

In Toronto, I immediately got married and landed as an immigrant. Living in a single room, dead broke, my wife and I went job hunting — desperately job hunting. I got onto an office position in a steel plant, purchasing desk. A work shirt and borrowed tie, $5 shoes — it was a long wait to that first pay check. And what mind-grinding work it was. Let no one say all office work is for spongers. That year and a half I felt my brain flow out my ears at night; the amount of shit paper work that passed my desk was phenomenal. My starting pay was $85 a week (before taxes), and that in rip-off Toronto. Even in the end I was only up to $115 a week.

Here again I was doing more than one man's work. The purchasing department had originally consisted of the manager, his junior, a secretary, and four purchasing agents. Despite the increase in work due to computerization (I've always found that computerization *increases* the work load. What it *decreases* is the work force, for the cost of the computers cuts sharply into company profit and something has to give: i.e. *you*). The secretary was now doing the job of one agent in addition to her own. After one old purchaser retired, I and the senior man did the work of three. But then we wore a tie and that made us better than the unionized (and higher paid) guys out in the structural steel yard.

It was not long after I began working there that I received my own personalized visit from the RCMP. An agent entertained me one lunch break outside in a car, checking out the validity of certain lies they had received about me from the FBI.

140

With two fellow Wobblies from Montreal I started doing IWW agitational work and building up a branch in town. At that time out in Vancouver a young British immigrant kid had signed his construction crew mates into the IWW, but the Socred provincial labour board vetoed our union certification bid. Seems the IWW is not a "trade union under the meaning of the Act."

If anyone wonders why Wobblies have always been anarchists at heart, it is precisely through the kind of view they, by hard experience, gather of the State apparatus. Reliance on 'direct action' by the worker at the point of production is not an idea cooked up in some professor's head. It is the primary means whereby the worker gets what he needs. The experience of any worker in a strike action will tell him/her that. It is not arbitration by "just and impartial" minds, but rather the implied or real threat of working class violence that finally persuades the capitalist or his State tools to settle an argument to the worker's better gain.

Most workers know that instinctively. The primary task of radicals in North America, however, is to convince workers that it is possible to take this to its most logical conclusion. And that is the total removal of the capitalist and the State, with industry run by worker-elected union councils.

Rather than some obscure text from the Holy Fathers of Bolshevism, what the working person needs is the solid example of just how solidarity and mutual aid among workers can effect that change. Of course, workers that we ourselves are, broke and with our own individual cares and pressures, we have to start small and the examples are themselves but a microcosm of the whole. But a beginning has to be made somewhere.

As in my case. First of all, my own cares and worries: I was working at a button factory, chained to a machine and watching for quality control on touchy plastic. It was pretty boring work, punching out lapel pins, but delicate too, as the liquid plastic had to enter the cold steel die at just the right temperature and pressure — and left only long enough to harden before being quickly snapped out. I was the only male, working along with immigrant girls: Greek, Portuguese, Italian, Chinese, West Indian, etc. The women's task was even more difficult, as their more slender fingers, at a very fast pace (production en masse), fitted the tiny needles which served as clasps into minute holes in the dies. And too, I got to walk around occasionally, to check out supply and quality of plastic pellets. Which meant that I was paid 50c more an hour (for a grand $2.50).

I worked nights. Come morning I did picket duty as a supporter at the Artistic Strike in North York. Vicious police attacks resulted in 118 arrests. Six arrests were against Wobblies, for a total of twelve charges, mostly of common assault on police. Our people received the worst jail sentences and fines of any group on the strike lines. The small striking CTCU, affiliated to the nationalist Council of Canadian Unions, which vaunts itself as the great alternative to American AFL-CIO business unionism, refused to help anyone but its own — and their university strike leaders were given the better legal aid and courtroom support than the poor immigrant strikers who faced the loss of their jobs if convicted (as some were).

The CTCU couldn't even galvanize its own CTCU shops for support or pickets, let alone the wider CCU. We 'outsiders' were expected to be the cannonfodder, take the beatings, jailings and fines without a murmur and with not a word of say in how the picket lines were run. Our demand for a defense committee to raise legal aid from the community was rejected over and again by Stalinoid hacks Madeleine Parent and Kent Rowley, until, fearing that the rank-and-file supporters would start their own, they set up a paper front for a month with "safe" community figures on the project's mast-head. I was elected by the strike support committee along with a Trot and one independent moderate to join the defense group, but was vetoed by Parent. The 'defense group' was allowed to linger on for a month and then disbanded after not having raised a single penny for the arrested.

I had expected as much from the start, knowing full well that nationalists are always quick with the flag-waving but even quicker with the knife in the back. I had put out an appeal to Wobblies for help and in three months $2,500 came in, most in small bills from workers all over the world. Nearly $100 came in from Swedish IWW shipbuilders, another $100 from Wobbly workers on the Pacific island of Guam. All over Canada and the USA, and from Britain and Australia: working people helping us out with a few bucks. We had enough to cover our arrested Wobs and to aid a number of other hard-pressed strike supporters facing the Tory courts.

That was no one shot deal: as I write this I am raising funds for groups of anarchist workers in Spain and France who are being framed by the State, some even facing the garrotte — a barbaric medieval method of execution in which an iron collar is tightened around the neck until the spiked screw punctures or snaps the spinal cord, or strangulation occurs, whichever first. On March 2, 1974, Salvador Puig Antieh, a 26 year old anarchist in the Iberian Liberation Movement was murdered in such fashion in Spain... Already we have sent over $600 for legal defense; that may seem small, but there is no capitalist or Moscow gold involved. Just small donations from workers scattered around the world.

Mutual aid does work. We are proving it, on no matter how small the scale. Remember, that to the workers involved, it is sometimes even a matter of life itself.

Perhaps in this rambling account a glimmer is seen of just what forces can radicalize a worker. And how one such radicalized worker went from being an individualistic drifter to one working in collective effort with others of his class.

Oh, yes: I am working now as an oil test lab technician on the railroad. Earlier, as a labourer, I sweated my guts out on the engines. But I managed to land a laboratory job (less pay) in the same diesel shop. Working the grave-yard shift has given me a little spare time to write this article. If I were still a labourer, I doubt I'd have the time or energy to do it.

Letter to a Politician

Dear Sir, Toronto May 9, 1975

My name is "Frank Giancana", Canadian citizen. I also want you to remember that at the last election I voted for you and that I had your poster on my verandah. Now I want a favour. I want to know about the law in Canada that protects workers. I have been working since 1963 for Emanuel Products. I began working for $1.25 an hour. Now, 12 years later, the company has expanded. Has purchased two blocks. It has a plant in Preston and one in Queensview, with the blood of the Italians. In January we renewed our contract. Through the Union we got $1. for two years bringing the highest pay to $4.30 an hour and the lowest to $3.90. In concluding I would like to say for the past four months we have been mistreated, 100 workers were laid off and they expect that the same work be carried out by the number of workers left. They have brought in a person who stands at our backs and with a chronometer and then tells us that we should produce 60 pieces an hour or else "go home". We are now 150 workers and we work four days a week. There were 20 foremen before, there are 25 now. Instead of one with the chronometer we now have two. They stand at your back and they tell you: "you have to produce 30 pieces". If you produce 28 they will give you a red tag, the warning. In three days, a friend of mine who has worked there for 25 years has received 2 tags. The company pushes us now like horses. If you don't make 50 an hour you go home. We have spoken to the Union representatives who recommend that we make a grievance. It takes from 5 to 7 months for the Department of Labour to deal with a grievance and even then the decision is made in favour of those who have a lot of money. The worker never wins. On Thursday the — Union Chairman, the Steward and two workers were suspended indefinitely. It might be for a week or for a month. Members of the Union have learned about the fact that the President of the Company has told them: "either do that or go home" and they were suspended. The rest of the workers stopped working in protest. The company told us: "go away, you are all suspended". They called the police and locked the gates. The company has now sent us a letter to say that for each day of strike we have to pay a $100 fine. We have replied that we did not go on strike, we want that our colleagues be permitted to return to work. The company will not hear of it. Now I want to know why is there in Canada such descrimination. I have 3 children, a wife to support and a house to keep. Tell me how can I manage on my salary? If we have been useful for 20 years, how come we are no longer able to work? In Canada the law is in favour not of the worker, but of the rich. Why does not the Liberal government send an inspector to see the conditions under which we work and establish accordingly our wages. Only then we can say that this is democracy for all. Immigrants are taken advantage of, therefore we have a high number of accidents at work, because they cannot protect themselves against danger. Hope you will excuse me for writing such a long letter. But I believe that a person who for 15 years has not needed welfare or unemployment insurance is a good worker, but for Emanuel we are no longer any good. In Italy a person who works for twenty years for the same company is entitled to 10 milioni Lira in severance pay. Instead our company gives us the red tag. I thank you with all my heart for what you will be able to do for the Emanuel Products workers.

On behalf of 75 Italians who work for this company I send you our best regards,

"Frank Giancana"

"Frank Giancana" is a pen-name for a person working at Emanuel Products in Toronto. A pen-name is used to protect the worker from punitive actions by his present employer.

Towards a Working Class Radicalism in Canada: A Polemic

by Walter Johnson

In the past few years there has been growing concern about the proliferation of wildcat strikes, work stoppages, industrial sabotage and other such manifestations of "labour unrest". As a result there has been much heated debate and controversy about the problems of workers in modern industrial society. There is an endless stream of articles, films and books dealing with the working class as seen through the eyes of academicians, broadcast journalists and professional cause-pedlars. Under these circumstances it is inevitable that a particular viewpoint will prevail since the people analysing the working class are, with few exceptions, from the middle class or, at least, have middle class pretensions. During the thirties, when much of the middle class was uprooted and suffering, workers were portrayed as noble and stout-hearted fellows imbued with virtue and high-minded idealism. The failure of the economic system had impelled disinherited middle class intellectuals and workers to unite against the injustices of low wages, job insecurity and poor living conditions.

Many people believed that the union movement, with its aura of radicalism, was the best vehicle for a fundamental change in the social fabric. From the early experiences of the labour movement the idea arose that it might be possible to gradually transform capitalism into socialism by way of reforms. This idea appealed to intellectuals who suspected that the esoteric goals of ideology were not the prime concerns of the average man. The exploitation theory was, at least, relevant to the worker who could lose his job through the capricious whim of an employer or his managers, but any long range ideological goals seemed highly impracticable at the time. Even the Communist Party, the most conspicuously ideological group of the depression era, supported, at Moscow's behest, most reformist policies from 1935 to the end of the second World War.

The union movement flourished and with its growth came collective bargaining grievance procedures, and fringe benefits. The improvements diluted labour-management antagonisms and, as a consequence, the intellectual influence of radicals was eroded considerably. When it proved possible to improve working conditions within the confines of capitalism, the once radical labour movement became just another institution providing additional support for the social status quo.

The labour movement's alliance with radical elements was further weakened when the prosperity generated by World War II enabled disenfranchised intellectuals to re-enter the middle class world of government, universities, and the professions, thus depriving the unions of the ideological visions which were, although not acceptable to most workers, so influential in the thirties.

Structural changes in the capitalist system also undermined the radical imperative. Education competed with capital and the corporation was hatched with a technical and managerial elite that often included the children of the working class. The founding entrepreneurs were replaced by faceless managers and organization men and the shrewder corporate interests conceded that reforms were necessary in order to stave off a more radical transformation of society. Progressive managers, who had been influenced by the writings of industrial psychologists, discovered that by encouraging good labour-management relations the conflicts between union and management decreased markedly. The most prescient members of the national corporation class soon realized that if there was to be any kind of socialism at all, it must be corporate socialism, and this type of socialism must be administered from above.

Deprived of intellectual influence, the unions increasingly rejected ideological arguments culminating with the expulsion of Communist union members in the later forties. When it was discovered that the Communist Parties in North America had been acting as pawns for Russian foreign policy, many people became disillusioned and bitter about radicalism in general. To many people the Communists were proof that all radicalism was alien to this country and conspiratorial in nature.

Reformers, the liberal left, and many former radicals applauded the "pragmatism" of the anti-ideological purge. State capitalism had absorbed and/or institutionalized the dissenting voices of the thirties and only a few unreconstructed anarchists and marxists resisted the change with any vigour. The middle class radicals of the thirties, who had been estranged from the more primitive pre-war economy, became the pillars of the post-war liberal technocratic establishment. The increasingly complex functions of administration and management both of the economy and of the society at large required a large bureaucratic stratum which could only be recruited from universities and other intellectual centres. Key people from the new managerial bureaucracies would be granted ruling class privileges if they could perform the invaluable service of muffling conflicts and facilitating the smooth and efficient functioning of the economy. The continued existence of the capitalist system depended, then, on its capacity to absorb and integrate dissident intellectuals into the existing social order. The new technocratic class had a decidedly liberal hue (which was no surprise considering its origins) and the idea arose that it might be possible, through state intervention, to re-order the basic economic priorities of the society and to favour the social rather than the free enterprise sector. This idea was also supported by the labour movement which, at that time, was consolidating the social and organizational gains of the thirties.

Thus the broader framework of radicalism was largely abandoned in favour of the "pragmatists" obsession with statism and power through electoralism. In the ensuing decades social dissenters were absorbed by the universities and, therefore, segregated from the mainstream of society. Social criticism became elitist, self-serving and irrelevant to the mass of industrial workers.

The working class became an easy target for criticism or ridicule when the liberal game plan didn't work. Within the span of three decades the noble worker of the thirties was miraculously transformed into the narrowminded, fearful bigot of the sixties. Films, books and t.v. programs began to depict workers as brutal, materialistic slobs. The oversimplified "Archie Bunker" blue collar stereotype identified bigotry and stupidity as the sole prerogative of the working class.

Young, middle class radicals of the sixties could not understand the reluctance of workers to join the ecology movement or anti-war, anti-poverty protests. The emergence of this blue collar conservatism also annoyed many old fashioned reformers and ex-radicals who felt betrayed by the grubby, ultra-materialistic working class. The schism widened when workers disdainfully rejected the anti-materialistic lifestyle of dissatisfied middle class offspring. The hysterical, anti-technological crusades of the sixties seemed absurd to workers who, for years, considered upward mobility a positive goal (since World War II real wages had been rising in well organised industries). It was paradoxical why so much sympathetic attention was given the young by the media and by those same intellectuals who had always extolled the virtues of the working class.

The hypocrisy of the situation was evident to most workers from the very beginning. Activists who berated the working class for being apathetic and cynical were very often the intellectual heirs of people who had deserted the working class struggle to carve out safe niches for themselves in the postwar technocracy. It was the reform minded liberals and ex-radicals who had opted for security (and the state) rather than press for a fundamental change of the society. When the disaffected children of the middle class picked up the torch their parents refused to carry, the working class was, understandably, skeptical of their motives. With the advantage of hindsight, it seems that this skepticism was justified. Many of the middle class radicals of the sixties have been only too willing to re-enter the mainstream lifestyle and assume roles and attitudes which they previously despised. When asked for the reason for their conversion, these ex-radicals often mention the failure of the working class to respond to a radical critique of society. Elitist radicals view the working class as the great unwashed, a heaving mass of humanity ready to be shaped and molded into the image that most corresponds with the latest utopian fantasy. Workers are, through necessity and bitter experience, more realistic in their aspirations, and they recoil from the high blown radical rhetoric which is so often and so easily betrayed.

It requires considerable effort for middle class radicals to divest themselves completely of the patronizing and holier-than-thou attitudes that seem to be a built-in feature of their genre. When writing or talking about the working class many of these so-called radicals unwittingly fluctuate between attitudes of condescension and exaggerated self-abasement. Nowhere is this more evident than in academia where the critical faculties are very often developed without the concomitant wisdom. For this reason, many workers are convinced that middle class, university centered radicalism is disingenuous and should be ignored.

The enormous changes wrought by technology have created an entirely new set of problems and frustrations for industrial workers and the campus radicals are, for the most part, unwilling or unable to understand the change. To begin with, the university itself is a contradiction between expressed goals and real purpose: the conflict between egalitarian justification and privileged practice, between state support and disestablishmentarianism, between disinterestedness and professional competition, between equal rating (to enlighten every citizen) and invidious rating (exclusion from entry, comparative grading, exclusion on academic grounds), between armchair dissent and public conformity. Much student radicalism stems from the realization that the actual purpose of the university is quite different from its avowed goals. If the radicalism spills over into a general critique of society it is very often tinged by a middle class perspective and thus seems insincere to a working class constituency which still believes that a university education grants people a privileged place in society.

It is, then, no less than a minor miracle if a university-spawned radical can establish genuine rapport with workers. Among workers there is always the lingering suspicion that university radicals are guilty of class betrayal and self-contempt. There is also the knowledge that middle class radicals have now become so dependent on institutions within the system that they are virtually powerless to effect any real change in the social order. Middle class dissenters usually end up working in the school system, the media, the civil service, the trade union bureaucracies, or some state supported community agency. The elitist nature of these institutions, and the fact that they are subsidized from the pockets of the productive sector of the economy, breeds a resentment among working class people that is often directed, unfortunately, at the people who work in these institutions rather than at the economic system which depends on these institutions for survival.

The result of this misdirected anger is a phony conflict between workers as taxpayers and other workers as tax supported public employees. People caught up in oppressive, state supported institutions are so busy protecting their own precarious positions that they are effectively hamstrung when radical action is needed. This is often the dilemma in which middle class radicals find themselves mired.

Workers are beginning to realize that advanced industrialized societies are impervious to change from above. The absorptive and co-optive capacity of State and monopoly capital has neutralized any threat to the status quo from middle class critics. The impetus for radical social change must emanate from rank and file agitation at the point of production.

In the past forty years the evolution of the trade union movement and the growth of the State have produced serious conflicts and divisions within the working class that militate against the development of a radical labour movement. There are conflicts between well paid workers in highly productive manufacturing concerns and poorly paid workers in the less productive service sector, between workers in the private sector and tax supported public employees, between trade union bureaucrats and informal underground unions, between taxpaying workers and unemployed workers or welfare recipients, between white collar and blue collar workers, and between male workers and the increasing female proportion of the labour force.

The existence of these conflicts, however, indicates that a severe social crisis is pending and that a working class unity on economic issues might eventually be forged. No society can long tolerate the type of internal strife which is now being manifested in North America. When workers in poorly paid public sector jobs go on strike for decent wages they incur the wrath and resentment of private sector workers who not only suffer a loss of service but also pay increased taxes to finance any wage gains made as a result of the strike. Unorganized and low paid workers are ravaged and left behind by the inflation that is generated when well organized workers negotiate high wage gains to compensate for the heavy tax burden the State foists on them. Economic demands by the recipients of welfare and unemployment insurance funds cause resentment among better paid workers who help to finance these programs through taxes.

Well paid workers also help to finance the schools and colleges that absorb the unemployable labour of hundreds of thousands of young people. Through taxes workers pay for the investment by the State in expensive highways that have underwritten the expansion of the structure of private investment in automobiles. This also benefits, directly or indirectly, other industries in the monopolized sector that depend on the automobile industry. Workers in the monopolized private sector are part of the labour aristocracy: the most productive and highly paid segment of the economy. Since the end of the Second World War workers in the labour aristocracy have been told by trade union leaders that they have a stake in the profits and prosperity of business. As long as real wages increased, workers did not object to heavy taxation to subsidize their employers, but when real wages remained the same or declined, the effects were explosive. Over the past twenty years the State subsidy to monopoly private capital has been so great that a major distortion of the economy has taken place. Until recently it was workers outside the highly paid sector who, through low wages, unemployment or underemployment, bore the brunt of economic stagnation and the concentration of capital in a few large industries. Since the late sixties the job crisis has spread and now threatens to engulf workers in the highly paid sector as well.

The erosion of purchasing power, loss of job security, and increased taxes have forced previously quiescent workers to adopt a more militant stance in relationship to both the company they work for and to the State. The cost of absorbing the job crisis caused by economic stagnation puts the State and monopoly capital in an ever-tightening vise as higher taxes must be extracted from the productive sector to subsidize the burgeoning surplus labour no longer needed in direct manufacturing and service. Until now, this subsidy has been skillfully camouflaged in a number of ways: by encouraging higher educational requirements thereby postponing young people's entry into the labour market, by the expansion of teaching jobs to meet the expansion of education, by the development of the public service sector and the increase of poorly paid service jobs in the private sector, by the unemployment or underemployment of immigrants and the chronically poor.

The job crisis could only remain hidden as long as the real wages of well paid workers in the highly productive sector increased. In the past few years real wages have fallen, unemployment has increased, and inflation has reached epidemic proportions. The debt structure in the private sector is collapsing and, as a consequence, small company bankruptcies are more common. Personal indebtedness is on the upsurge and the quality of life, especially in the cities, has deteriorated rapidly. The price of decent housing has skyrocketed and now even the middle class is suffering from the housing shortage.

The first casualties of the job crisis are the working poor. The working poor are people who do not belong to rich, highly organized unions or special interest groups. Workers in small shops and factories, hospital workers, dishwashers, cabdrivers, waitresses, gas station attendants, janitors, farm labourers and other service people comprise a major portion of the group. The jobs done by the working poor are socially useful and resist automation yet they are often, paradoxically, the worst paying. Working conditions are usually substandard and living costs are high.

The working poor are a new strata of dispossessed citizens who function at the periphery of the highly organized, technological society. It is a disturbing contrast to the special interest groups in our society, who have knowledgeable and articulate spokesmen to voice their concerns.

Private scholars, academics, and unemployed youngsters of the middle class are eligible for government support programs (LIP, OFY, Canada Council, etc.). Government assistance is also available to companies in undeveloped areas (DREE) and tax deferrals are considered a business necessity. Tax deferrals for individuals (RRSP, RHOSP, interest and divident deductions) allow high income professionals and sub-professionals, who have discretionary income, to contribute to these plans, to enhance their security and privileged place in society. Semi-monopolistic unions and companies can obtain inflated salaries for their employees and adequate compensation during lay-offs (unemployment benefits are more easily obtained and the payments are generous. There are also a variety of supplementary unemployment benefit schemes which have become popular in some industries).

The highly organized and educated have, in effect, been subsidized while the working poor compete for jobs which are low paying and demeaning by middle class standards. To the people excluded from the educational and industrial elite, life becomes an unrelenting grind as food, rent and other basic expenses rise uncontrollably.

It is therefore understandable that the working poor view the government as an elitist institution operating for the benefit of the middle class. "Liberal" intellectuals decry the propensity to conservatism that is often evident among low income people. Much of this so-called conservatism is really a reaction to policies and programs which seem designed to consolidate the power of the middle class while ignoring the economic problems of the unorganized, uneducated, and unrich.

The working poor, however, are no longer willing to remain complacent in the face of rampant inflation and government inaction. Discontent is now surfacing through citizens' action groups and other grass roots organizations that attempt to mobilize people on the basis of shared problems and frustrations. In these new groups, there is less reliance on middle class community organizers and more emphasis on quiet, long term educational programs that develop class consciousness. Gone are the frequent meetings and public confrontations that enabled publicity hungry career "radicals" to gain notoriety and benefit personally but did little to improve the lives of the working poor.

The new approach favours political education about the history and sociology of the working class interfused with practical activity around relevant issues. There is no desire to involve the working poor in a premature struggle with powerful institutions which can only result in humiliation and defeat. Every effort is made to develop a broad based coalition linking local groups to a strong overall organization. This is accomplished by studying the class nature or universality of certain issues, thus transcending merely parochial concerns and enabling people to identify with working class elements elsewhere. In this way a genuine class-oriented radicalism is being engendered among the working poor.

In sharp contrast to the working poor are the well organized and highly paid tradesmen and workers in the large scale manufacturing concerns: the beneficiaries of forty years of trade union activity and influence. For this "labour aristocracy" the bread and butter issues, so important to the working poor, have been supplanted by concern about the very nature of the work itself. Workers are faced with methods and work conditions that are increasingly unbearable. The work process has become so fragmented and routinized that workers are reduced to mere appendages of the machine. As a consequence, there is mounting shop floor dissatisfaction which reveals itself through absenteeism, shoddy workmanship and sabotage. In some factories, informal underground unions have been formed to deal with issues and problems that the established union structure ignores. The old-fashioned unions, geared to deal with specific wage and benefit demands, are incapable of redressing the less tangible in-plant grievances such as job frustration, nervous exhaustion and the despotic behaviour of supervisory personnel.

Most workers now realize, instinctively, that the traditional union is not always the best vehicle for basic change since, in many cases, the approved procedures are woefully inadequate to deal with new problems. To sufficiently cope with job frustrations, unions would have to recognize that the goals of the rank and file workers and the goals of the corporation they work for are not coterminus. Most labour unions are now almost identical, structurally, to the managerial hierarchies of the large corporations. Union leaders have become bureaucrats or "labour statesmen" far removed from the daily concerns of the rank and file. As a result, the growing shop floor discontent is directed not only against management but also against the centralized and bureaucratic union leadership. This discontent, coupled with a deteriorating economy, could produce a politically explosive situation comparable to the social upheavals of the thirties.

Since World War II workers in the labour aristocracy have usually been safe from the ravages of unemployment, but lately they have discovered that their immunity is only relative. The spreading job crisis has affected some workers who have never before experienced a prolonged period of unemployment. Unlike the working poor, who are often outside of unions and have little political power, the labour aristocracy is capable of exerting considerable political pressure when widespread lay-offs occur. If the renewed militancy of rank and file workers is any indication, this political pressure might contain a radical element which, since the thirties, has been sadly lacking in the Canadian labour movement.

Much has been written about the resistance of Canadian workers to concepts like workers' control, industrial democracy and self-management. It is argued that these concepts are European in origin and somehow inappropriate to the business unionism of the Canadian labour movement. Another argument often advanced is that Canadian workers are basically conservative, like their American counterparts, and are fearful of any change which might threaten their standard of living. Such simple minded explanations are nothing more than the verbal diarrhea of sell-out unionists and the intellectual apologists who see no harm in American domination of the Canadian economy.

Workers in branch plant industries are wary of change because of their dependence on the American economy. It is absurd to talk about workers' control and industrial democracy when most of a firm's important manufacturing processes are located in a foreign country. Canadian workers realize that, under the present conditions, they are little more than an updated, industrialized version of the hewers of wood and drawers of water who have played such an important role in our folklore. Along with any movement towards workers' control there must also be a national industrial strategy to regain control of the national economy for Canadians.

In the past few years there has been a growing militancy among white collar workers in Canada. The downgrading and mechanization of clerical skills has produced a new breed of office workers who, much like their counterparts in the factory, are fed up with job monotony, factory-like supervision, phoney office politics and socialization, and an ever-decreasing control over their work environment. Bank tellers, typists, computer operators, stock clerks, mail sorters, payroll and time keeping clerks, telephone operators, shipping and receiving clerks, file clerks, bookkeepers, and many others are increasingly subjected to fragmented routines that strip them of the ability to understand whole processes, to use judgement or make decisions. By reducing mental

156

labour to a repetitive performance of the same small set of functions, there has been a progressive elimination of thought from the activities of clerical workers. Brainwork is still involved but the brain functions in much the same way as the hand of the factory production worker, dealing with familiar patterns over and over again. (The worst example of this process has been in computer technology which, for most people involved, has deteriorated from a potential craft requiring an extensive knowledge of all machinery and processes to just another production job with a division of labour resembling factory work.)

The growth, factory-like rationalization and subsequent division of labour of office work has eroded many of the advantages, securities and higher pay scales that, at one time, caused clerical workers to identify their interests with those of management. There has also been an influx of people from working class backgrounds who are not at all impressed by the dubious prestige claims that have traditionally separated white collar workers from the rest of the working class. Layoffs, low pay, insecurity and a growing feeling of impotence has forced many clerical workers to recognize their real class position in society. As a result, white collar unionism has gained support and is open to the influence of more traditional working class unions and the radical ginger groups which they now contain.

Finally, there is the rapidly expanding public service sector of the economy. People in this group include social workers, garbagemen, prison guards, teachers, clerks, lower level civil servants, and employees of custodial institutions such as senior citizen's homes, juvenile detention centres and workshops for the handicapped.

Workers in the public service sector are increasingly dissatisfied with low wages and the often ambiguous nature of their work. Ostensibly, their job is to help people but, in reality, they are very often performing a social control function by concealing the failures of society and acting as a conduit for the frustrations of the chronically poor, the marginal work force and the socially misfit. Now it is their task to patch up the problems created by the job crisis and the resulting social breakdown. Rather than remain the bandaid brigade of capitalism many public service workers are now determined to function in the best interests of the working class and not the corporate community. If this idea gains ascendancy there is, at least, a chance that public and private workers can be brought together in a radical coalition. If, on the other hand, the objectives of public service workers are merely economic and self-serving there will be a divisive backlash from private sector workers who are already burdened by an excessive tax load.

Workers in the public sector are engaged in non-profit labour and must depend on the State to pay their salaries. During an economic crisis or recession government budgets must be tightened to compensate for the dwindling tax base in the private sector. When the government attempts to hold down the wages of a particular group of public service workers, there is almost unanimous opposition from other public service groups since they all share the same employer and eventually must re-negotiate their own contracts. Because of this unity of interests, a tremendous radical potential already exists in the public sector. If the new radicalism becomes too narrowly defined it will be easy to anta-gonize private sector workers and foster the phoney class enmity which the State and corporate interests thrive on.

It must be realized that the State and the corporate community have a vested interest in perpetuating the tensions that separate the working poor, the labour aristocracy, and the public service workers into hostile camps. Only in a job crisis, such as the one occurring now, are the articifial barriers between working class groups weakened and the arbitrary power of the State and the multinational corporations re-vealed. The current economic crisis affects workers from all these groups and provides a new opportunity for the development of a broad-based working class radicalism in Canada.

There is much evidence to suggest that this broadbased working class radicalism will exhibit a strong libertarian socialist orientation. In recent years workers have demonstrated a genuine revulsion not only to management and the trade union bureaucracy but also to the many old-left type groups which have been resurrected to fill the vacuum left by the failure of the new left and counterculture. All the tired, shop-worn slogans of the authoritarian left are now being heard by a new generation of industrial workers. Among workers there is a widespread antipathy to the efforts of these re-cycled nostrum pedlars and ideologi-cal hacks now crouching at the periphery of the labour movement. Workers have been most receptive to the idea of radical self-organiza-tion at the point of production. Worker militancy on the shop floor is the most relevant form of protest and, if firmly rooted, the most dif-ficult for management and the union to control or co-opt. It is also the kind of struggle which creates new allegiances, promotes free discus-sion and exhange among the rank and file, and paves the way to a better understanding of the industrial system and, by extension, the society at large. What is now lacking among rank and file militants is a clear radical vision which transcends the usual reform demands and poses a concrete alternative not only to the way the workplace is or-ganized but also to the way the society is organized. It is in this area that intellectuals of the libertarian socialist persuasion can make the greatest contribution. By acting as animators and resource people rather than as "leaders" they can provide insurgent rank and file committees or radical working class affinity groups with the intellectual ammunition (theory, historical perspectives and precedents, intellectual justification) required to create a truly free society. This is not as impossible as it sounds. As

John Case has pointed out, "the problem of posing an alternative, then, must be faced sooner or later: if we are serious about the need for basic change, we must begin the discussion now."

In Spain for forty years before the Civil War anarchist clubs and unions debated the nature of the society they sought to build. They asked — and began to answer — questions of how a producer controlled economy might operate, how national planning and coordination could be accomplished democratically, how they would stimulate education and individual development. When the Civil War brought the collapse of the old social order, anarchists in Catalonia were able to replace existing economic and political institutions with their own, which were established in accordance with the principles that they had so carefully developed. And though the experiment was ultimately smashed by the Loyalist government and the Communists, it proved remarkably successful during its short life." It is this type of clear radical vision which is desperately lacking in the Canadian labour movement at present. To be sure, there have been signs that Canadian workers are more than ready to move beyond the traditional collective bargaining and picket line process. To resolve outstanding grievances many workers have resorted to direct action by staging wildcat strikes or by sabotaging expensive machinery. During one lengthy strike at United Aircraft in Montréal union strategy evolved to the point where a physical occupation of plant facilities was considered by the union leadership (see interview with Jean Marie Gonthier) and actually carried out by rank and file militants. Activities of this kind are an expression of militancy on a certain level but, taken alone, they do very little to bring about real social change. Without a social vision, acts of this nature can become shabby, egotistical outbursts closely resembling the random, purposeless violence now seen so frequently in the large cities. The vision that remains the most compatible to the liberal-democratic traditions of Canadian workers is a society of self-government and self-management; a society in which workers collectively determine what they produce, how they produce it, and how their product will be distributed. The first step in achieving this kind of society is the demand for control of the work environment. When workers make their own decisions concerning the pace, methods and conditions of work they are but one step away from control of the enterprise itself. Other demands might include the right to control all pension and insurance funds, access to all corporate financial records, the right to veto management on all pricing and production policies, the right to organize factory committees, the right to publish and distribute any literature emanating from the factory committees (see Assembly — line Merry-go-round). Every effort should be made to gain control of the decision making process. In this way workers acquire knowledge, new skills and the expertise required to eventually run the enterprise themselves. More importantly, a spirit of cooperation and mutual aid is engendered making hierarchical and competitive division of labour seem grossly absurd (see the interview with Jean Levesque). There are some demands, such as voluntary overtime, shortened workweek, longer breaks, higher wages, better fringe benefits, which are useful but which can be easily incorporated into a management governed workers participation scheme. A great deal of energy can be expended in achieving these demands while the prerogatives of management and private capital remain unchallenged. Control of the work environment must be the primary demand in any workers' control strategy. The demands formulated should attempt to maximize the autonomous power of workers at the base, to promote a feeling of efficacy, and to legitimize the concept of workers' self-management of the means of production. The culmination of this workers' control strategy is the totally self-managed firm in which the workers are the primary governing body. Once workers effectively control an enterprise the problems of in-plant organization become crucial. Rank and file committees could be created, each responsible for some facet of production, distribution, and maintenance. Responsibilities would be shared by the committees on a rotating basis thus avoiding a monopoly on expertise from developing in any particular area. Delegates to factory committees would be elected democratically, rotated regularly to different committees, and subject to instruction and recall from below. Open committee meetings would be held (see the interviews with Jean Levesque and Claude Petelle) to allow workers the maximum participation in the day to day operations of the enterprise. To constantly invigorate the base and to prevent the development of a bureaucratic mentality, delegates could not be elected to consecutive terms on the factory committees. Rank and file workers would be encouraged to take the initiative, to act for themselves, and to build co-operation voluntarily. The goal would be a work environment where individual responsibility is paramount and a feeling of mutual reciprocal obligation among workers the norm.

Having gone this far, it is unlikely that workers would be content to settle for self-management of industry without some form of community control or self-government as well. Try to envisage the following scenario: Working together, the local industry and the community could provide social services such as health, education, recreation, municipal transportation and the provision of utilities. Workers would democratically control the workplace but any important economic decisions would require the participation of the entire community. The social unit would be inclusive of all the people — the young, the old, the infirm, the indigent — and not just the highly "productive" factory workers. Every effort would be made to prevent the formation of groups whose special interests ran counter to the interests of the broader community. Individual privacy and the rights of minorities would have to be protected. A new definition of the role of women in the community would be essential. All important issues would be hammered out by workers' committees and local councils. Delegates or representatives of local councils or assemblies might then meet to form regional councils based on geographic contiguity. Regional councils would be responsible for co-ordinating the production and distribution of goods and services between communities within the region. On a national scale these regional councils might federate to co-ordinate economic activities and resist American imperialism. Representatives to regional councils and a national federation would be strictly mandated and subject to immediate recall by their communities. The primary task of representatives would be to encourage local action and popular initiative to solve problems. The goal of such a society would be the elimination of the distinctions between the private (economic) sphere and the public (political) sphere. All activities would be subject to democratic control thus making problems such as educational reform, regional economic disparities, and environmental pollution easier to identify, isolate and deal with.

The possibilities for a radical social alternative are endless but the impetus for such a change must originate in the community and at the workplace. There is a wide range of tactical alternatives available to workers to bring about change. Insurgent rank and file unions present the biggest threat to both management and the union hierarchy because they do not engage in the collective bargaining process and thus cannot be compromised on important issues. Working within the established union framework can also be useful if the purpose is to help legitimize rank and file demands and the concept of self-management. Extra-union political organizations, like the League of Revolutionary Black Workers in the United States, have had some success in mobilizing workplace discontent. Small working class affinity groups can provide a much needed intellectual input into shop floor struggles. Many affinity groups have descended from tavern bull sessions where beefing and griping has been supplanted by a sophisticated understanding of industrial society and its political dynamics. Other workers have been successful in rallying community support for issues which affect everyone. Social workers join "clients" in attempts to reform the operations of social welfare departments. Hospital workers make alliances with community groups to improve working conditions in the hospital and, as a result, the level of health care in the community. Teachers, students, school boards and parents band together to push for decent salaries and a more personalized educational milieu. White collar workers unionize and begin to view themselves as part of the working class. Previously unorganized workers see the gains that can be made by joining together in common fronts and industry wide strikes. By striking an entire industry rather than a few small companies workers could finally put an end to the small, marginal shops which rely on cheap labour to survive.

A wide array of tactics can be used to bring about radical change. But the aim of such tactics should always be a radical transformation in all human relations. Until workers actually control their work environment and their institutions, no genuine social transformation is possible. Nothing worthwhile can be accomplished without a struggle. It is only through struggle that workers can realize their potential for self-organization and self-determination. It is a process which quickly dissolves the caked on layers of cynicism, apathy, and passivity acquired through years of inactivity and resignation. To regain control of our lives and to rediscover a sense of destiny might seem like an impossible dream to some workers but, as Max Weber said, it is only by pursuing the impossible that we will make what is possible come true.

THE POLITICS OF OBEDIENCE:

The Discourse of Voluntary Servitude

by Etienne de la Boetie

This classic work of political reflection seeks the answer to the question of why people submit to the tyranny of governments. La Boétie laid the groundwork for the concept of civil disobedience with his proposal that people could cut the bonds of habit and corruption that keep them obedient and complacent, and resolve to serve their masters no more. The *Discourse of Voluntary Servitude* has exerted an important influence on the tradition of pacifism and civil disobedience from Thoreau and Ralph Waldo Emerson, to Tolstoy, to Gandhi.

Etienne de la Boétie was a sixteenth century political philosopher and a close friend of Montaigne.

"(La Boétie's) analysis of tyranny and his insight into its psychological foundations ought to be one of the central documents in the library of anyone concerned with human liberty. It is ironic that the works of Machiavelli, advisor to rulers, should enjoy widespread currency, while the libertarian La Boétie is muted. Hopefully, publication of his 1550 *Discourse*, with its superb introduction by Murray Rothbard, will right the imbalance."

— Stanley Milgram
author of *Obedience to Authority*

88 pages / Hardcover $10.95 / Paperback $2.95
ISBN: 0-919618-58-8 / ISBN: 0-919618-57-X

Contains: Canadian Shared Cataloguing in Publication Data

DEMOCRACY AND THE WORK PLACE

by Harold B. Wilson

"A book which might conceivably be the most single useful volume ever produced for the modern socialists of Canada."
— Douglas Fisher, *Toronto Sun*

"Another recent book that should be read... Wilson provides the Canadian orientation... but he also goes beyond the philosophical approach to show how industrial democracy can be achieved..."
— Ed Finn, *Toronto Daily Star*

"Even though they might not like what they read, corporation managers should run out and buy a copy. They might then be partially prepared if the socialist hordes break down the door."
— George Dobie, *Vancouver Sun*

"...It may well become a classic of socialist literature."
— Roy LaBerge, *The Courier*

"We have been waiting for a long time for a book which deals constructively with the world of work which most Canadians experience in their daily life. For Canadians this has been a neglected subject. Harold Wilson's book is an important exception. It is timely, relevant and controversial."
— Gerry Hunnius, Atkinson College, York University

267 pages | Hardcover $10.95 | Paperback $3.95
ISBN: 0-919618-23-5 / ISBN: 9-919618-22-7

Chosen for *Canadian Basic Books*

CANADA
AND RADICAL
SOCIAL CHANGE

edited by
Dimitrios
Roussopoulos

This collection of outstanding essays on various
social questions in Canada are taken from the radical
quarterly journal, OUR GENERATION which was
founded in 1961. The journal, which has the highest
circulation among the publications of this type in the
country, has made a lasting contribution to the
serious discussion concerning the Canadian social
crisis.

The essays deal with unemployment, youth
politics, poverty, economic continentalism, the new
left, urban renewal, electoralism, and parliamentary
democracy, and the student revolt.

Contributors include some of our most outstanding
commentators: Fred Caloren, B. Roy Lemoine,
Philip Resnick, Gerry Hunnius, George Grant, Jim
Harding, Evelyn Dumas, Mel Watkins, Jim Laxer,
Christian Bay, and many others.

250 pages | Hardcover $10.95 | Paperback $2.95
ISBN: 0-919618-10-3 / ISBN: 0-919618-09-x

Chosen for *Canadian Basic Books*

THE STATE

by Franz Oppenheimer

Introduction by
C. Hamilton

"Oppenheimer took the best insights from the conflict school in Europe in his time and applied them, with much imagination and learning, to his study of the political state. I have long regarded it as a classic and welcome its fresh publication. I hope it will be read widely by the generation of social scientists, too many of whom have become nurtured by consensus theories of the state."

— Robert Nisbet

"Oppenheimer's *The State* merits the status of a classic of sociology and political science. Although his theory was linked to rather naive proposals for reform, and although some historical details may be inexact, its broad thesis remains true: namely that large-scale systems of power have originated from conquest and functioned as means of exploitation. The book helps us to realize how recent, precious and fragile are the ideas and institutions of democracy and welfare state."

— Stanislav Andreski

122 pages / Paperback $3.95
ISBN: 0-919618-59-6

BLACK ROSE BOOKS No. E 21

THE BITTER THIRTIES IN QUEBEC

by Evelyn Dumas
translated by
Arnold Bennett

Evelyn Dumas is one of Québec's best known journalists. She pioneered reporting on the labour movement while working for *Le Devoir,* was an Associate Editor with the *Montreal Star* and now works with *Le Jour.*

With this her first book, she has undertaken to prove incorrect the notion previously held widely that the labour movement militancy associated with modern Québec was a feature born in the post-World War 11 period. By examining, through the tradition of oral history, several strikes in the thirties and forties in transportation, textiles and other important industries, and by recording the impressions and feelings of some of the surviving strikers whether leaders or rank-in-file militants, she captures the mood of the period. The book is a fine example of social history, and in fact rewrites the history of a whole period.

"The publisher... (has) done (us) a service by providing... this version of Evelyn Dumas' history. ... (The author), in bridging this... gag has provided an easy... introduction to a period of Quebec labour history... (which) is helpful background for... the equally bitter, seventies."

The Labour Gazette

"...The Bitter Thirties... can be as enjoyable reading as a good adventure story, albeit with far more substance.
...Thoroughly factual, yet written in lively journalistic style."

The Globe and Mail

175 pages | Hardcover $10.95 | Paperback $3.95
ISBN: 0-919618-53-7/ISBN: 0-919618-54-5

Contains: Canadian Shared Cataloguing in Publication Data

BLACK ROSE BOOKS No. E 19

LESSONS OF THE SPANISH REVOLUTION
BY VERNON RICHARDS

The struggle in Spain (1936-39) which was provoked by the rising military, aided and abetted by wealthy landowners and industrialists as well as by the Church, has generally been regarded in progressive circles outside Spain as a struggle between fascism and democracy, the latter being represented by the Popular Front government which had been victorious in the general elections of February 1936. Such an interpretation is the narrowest possible.

It was the revolutionary movement in Spain — the syndicalist movement — which took up Franco's challenge on July. 19, 1936 not as supporters of the Popular Front government but in the name of social revolution. This book is about the revolution, and the lessons to be drawn from it.

045 / 240 pages / Paperback $3.95 / $7.95 Hardcover

ANARCHISM AND ANARCHO-SYNDICALISM
BY RUDOLF ROCKER

Rocker gave his best years to the Jewish workers in the East End of London. He was born in Mainz, Germany in March 1873. Not only did he learn Yiddish but he also edited a Yiddish paper the *Arbeiter Freund* and a monthly *Germinal*. His writings are largely unknown in English because most of his writings were contributed to the German and Yiddish anarchist and syndicalist press. It is noteworthy however that his writings have been widely translated into Spanish for circulation in Latin America. This book is consider a classic.

046 / 48 pages / Paperback $1.75

Printed by
the workers of
Editions Marquis, Montmagny, Que.
for
Black Rose Books Ltd.